The Angel of Lygon Street

and other Poems of the Bizarre

by

David Lewis Paget

BARR BOOKS

For my friends at the Dinosaurs Club
The Copper Triangle Writers Group
For your fellowship
And your coffee

Other Poetry available by the author:

Pen & Ink — The Complete Works 1968-2008
Timepieces — The Narrative Poetry
At Journey's End — The Narrative Poetry, Vol. II
The Demon Horse on the Carousel — and Other Gothic Delights
Poems of Myth & Scare
The Devil on the Tree — and Other Poems of Dysfunction
Tales from the Magi
Taking Root
The Storm and the Tall Ship Pier
The Book on the Topmost Shelf
Tall Tales for Tired Times
Butterflies
The Widow of Martin Black
Goblin Dell
The Season of the Witch
Smugglers Pie
My China — Poetry in and about China
The Red Knight — Selected Poems

Foreword

Once more I offer a collection of intriguing, disparate poems, all narratives, about people and events that might well be real if I had not plucked them from that mystical storehouse of the imagination, and spattered them onto the page like a veritable, textual Blue Poles. Readers invariably ask me where these stories come from, and I can only answer them with a shrug. I am as bemused as they are.

All I can say with any certainty is that whenever the urge comes upon me, I have absolutely no idea what I'm going to write about. A line or two might suggest itself to me, either for the beginning or the ultimate end of the piece, and as long as the correct syllabic content is there I begin to work with it, allowing those initial lines to suggest whatever it is that will follow on, and in that way the poem begins to aid in its own construction. The storyline develops despite my worst intentions, and may take me on a rambling discourse far and away from what is initially intended.

But this is the beauty of working with rhyme and meter. The artificial constraints I put upon myself revolve around finding the correct rhyme, and many a storyline has veered away from the original conception due to the lack of a rhyming word.

So enjoy these flights of fancy. The characters may resemble people you know, or others that you're glad you don't. But as each tale unravels, you may find your own imagination pleasantly stimulated, and that's what makes it all worthwhile.

David Lewis Paget   April 2017

Contents

The Angel of Lygon Street

Back in the days of the old gas lamps
When the streets were lit, but dim,
A young lamplighter would tour the streets
And the houses, looking in,
The flickering flame of each lamp would light
The windows in the dark,
He'd see what he wasn't meant to see
In the light of each flickering spark.

He saw what he thought was an angel
Through a window in Lygon Street,
Sitting in front of a mirror,
Looking down, and washing her feet.
Her hair trailed over her shoulders like
Some golden ears of corn,
Then she looked up, and her bright blue eyes
Made him feel he was new-born.

Her lips were set in a steady pout
And were red and ripe to kiss,
Her brows were raised as she looked his way
And his heart felt instant bliss,
While she looked through her window pane
At the face of an angel boy,
Who, breathing mist on her window glass
Had scribbled his name there, 'Roy'.

Their eyes had locked with each other when
He framed his lips in a kiss,
And she stood up and approached him,
Then she put her lips to his,

They stayed so long that the glass had warmed
But the mist spread round about,
Till neither could see the other it
Had blotted each vision out.

Then every night he had lingered there
With his taper to her lamp,
And shivered out on the footpath for
The nights were getting damp,
He hoped that she would be sitting where
She had sat, before the kiss,
But nothing had moved within that room
From that day until this.

He didn't know but she'd had to go
To stay on her uncle's farm,
To breathe the purer air out there
Than the fog that did her harm,
She still spat blood in her handkerchief
But she thought about the boy,
Who'd kissed her once through a window pane
And the thought still brought her joy.

The One-Eyed Witch

Lavern lived down in the valley
Away from the village folk,
She didn't want to be seen by them
Playing with eggs and yolk,
And skin of frog, an old dead dog
A toad and the eye of newt,
She only conjured them in the fog
When dressed in her birthday suit.

But I would see her abroad in the woods
From up in the old oak tree,
She flitted naked under a hood
Albeit most carelessly,
She liked to gather her toadstools there
And take her favourite bat,
Clinging onto her long, dark hair
And follow her magical cat.

The mushrooms grown in a Faery Ring
Were an ever present danger,
For goblins gathered them all themselves
For a goblin baby's manger,
She'd lost an eye in a goblin pie
When he reached on out and plucked it,
She got it back, but the dwarf was sly
In the sauce she'd used, he'd ducked it!

I didn't mind that she'd got one eye
For her thighs were well developed,
I thought I'd marry her, by and by,
Then she went with Rodney Mellop,

I wandered up to her window-sill
When I heard his sighs and moans,
I thought they must have been making love,
She was hanging up his bones.

I must admit that it calmed me down,
That it put a damper on it,
I'd watched him lie in her pot and drown
As she danced in a pretty bonnet,
His bones she pulled from the boiling stew
And made wind chimes from his femurs,
At night they sound like a xylophone
In a madhouse full of dreamers.

Curling Horns

He lived in the outer darkness where
You never could see him cry,
With only a lighted candle there
Whenever his eyes were dry,
But I knew him for an evil soul
A troll that waited for you,
To cast me off like a heap of dross
Which is what he'd want you to do.

So you only saw a handsome prince
A hero there in the light,
You told me about the good things that
Your friend had done in your sight,
But you couldn't see the curling horns
That sprouted out of his head,
Nor even the narrow, squinting eyes
Glowing at night, bright red.

Your image of him was of a lord
Born of a line so high,
While I knew him as a Beelzebub
Who flew in the evening sky.
He often fluttered above my yard
Flinging his barbs at me,
They cut and wounded and hit me hard
With never you there to see.

I felt you slipping away from me
When I saw you huddled with him,
Whispering secret messages
In the hall of the local gym,
I knew that I'd have to take him out
Or risk the loss of your love,
So fashioned a wooden arrow for
One night, when he flew above.

I thought that I'd planned it perfectly
The crossbow hidden outside,
He fluttered over the garden wall
Looking for you, my bride,
I shot him straight through the heart with it,
His chest exploded in light,
I saw, on you, when you bent to him
Your curling horns in the night.

In My Mother's Wardrobe

The things that I'm going to tell you
Are secrets from childhood's well,
You must seal your lips from retelling
Or spend a season in hell,
In the back of my mother's wardrobe
Were some magical woods and a lake,
I'd creep on in to explore them
Whenever she wasn't awake.

I could tell by the way she was breathing
As she lay in a huddle in bed,
That she wasn't about and deceiving
As she did when her eyes were red,
I'd carefully turn the wardrobe key
And open the door, ajar,
The hinges would creak, my mother would speak
And say, 'I know where you are!'

I'd scuttle on into the wardrobe
And tumble right into a stream,
The water was dry, I didn't know why,
I guess it was simply a dream,
I'd get so entangled in stockings,
In corsets and silk underwear,
That I couldn't hear her open the door
And tell me 'I knew you were there!'

I think back on what I remember
And one of those things was the smell,
She had all these perfumes and lipsticks
And one that I know was Chanel,

But most I remember her diving
Headlong through the door, crying 'Heck!'
And dragging me out of her underwear
Each time, by the scruff of my neck!

London Train

In one of those fogs of London
I boarded the East End train,
The mist was a yellow, evil smog
And then it began to rain.
I found a compartment, only two
To bother my peaceful ride,
And placed my case at my feet, in place
With my gold-blocked name outside.

The smell of the fog was drifting in
And burning my eyes and throat,
I said to the man, 'Let fresh air in...'
He sat and buttoned his coat.
'The air out there is as bad as in,'
He said with a scowl and stare,
'*You* might be happy to sit and choke,
The window stays up, I swear.'

I leant well back, and looked at the girl
Who sat there, opposite me,
She wore her skirt right up to the hip,
I stared at her stockinged knee,
Her eyes were bright, an emerald green
But tears I saw on her cheek,
'This fog,' she muttered, and wiped them dry,
'I think it was worse last week.'

'But London's always suffered from fog,'
I ventured, 'Back in the day,
The Ripper used it to hide his crimes,
He used it getting away.'
'Overblown,' he said, the man in the coat,
'There's many was worse than he,
The blood ran thick in the gutters here
At times in our history.'

'But he's the one who never got caught,
You must at least give him **that**.'
The man slunk down in his corner seat,
Then sat, and played with his hat.
The girl just smiled, and said in a while,
I think you're right, he's the one,
I wouldn't like, on a foggy night
To meet him, minus a gun.'

The man reached into his overcoat
And seized the girl with a sigh,
Holding a cut-throat razor to
Her throat, with a smile so sly.
'I said I'd never do this again
But I must admit, I lied,
I noticed the name on your carry case,
You're Jekyll, I see – I'm Hyde!'

Demon Eyes

It hovered above on the ceiling,
It only would come at night,
My sister said she'd a feeling
It was dark, and was full of fright,
The light would glimmer and slowly fade
As the Moon came over the hill,
The globe grow dimmer in light and shade
Than a candle that flickered still.

I'd lie and I'd stare at the corner
Where the cloud had begun to swirl,
It had little form and no meaning
When first it began to unfurl,
But then came the claws in the ceiling
The eyes in the cloud glowing red,
And Clara would scream and be reeling
With her hands pulled over her head.

I thought that if I could disperse it,
It would run on back to its well,
And perhaps the Devil could curse it
Or find it a place in hell,
I beat at it with a baseball bat
But it seized the bat with its teeth,
And wrenched it out of my wretched hands
With a strength beyond belief.

It grew a cloak and a pair of horns
And roared with an orange flame,
It burnt a patch on the ceiling then
And I saw it had written its name,
'Askarametch' it had written there

The demon that lived in our well,
I said to Clara, 'it won't be long
I'll be sending the demon to hell.'

In daylight hours I filled up the well
With bracken and poisonous weeds,
Then as the sun was beginning to fade
I'd add Belladonna seeds,
A gallon of petrol damped it down
Till the Moon had begun to rise,
Then what I struck had it all lit up
To match the red demon's eyes.

We never see clouds on the ceiling now
It doesn't seem able to come,
The only thing is the sulphur smell,
It's potent, I give you the drum.
It drifts on in from the well outside
And hangs in the bedroom air,
While Clara sprays Devil's Nightcap for days,
It's better than demons in there.

Sleeping & Waking

That brief interlude between
Sleeping and waking,
I pass through each day like
Some dark undertaking,
Where nothing is real, where
I've been to or going,
My mind is disordered,
My heartbeat is slowing.

And even the room that I
Enter is swaying,
My eyes are distended my
Brain is nay-saying,
While legs stagger sideways
And crablike in function
Like some leaden corpse treated
To extreme unction.

The wars were all won, or
Were lost in the sleeping,
While everything worthwhile
Would seem to be weeping,
The slate should be cleared by
Each act of purgation,
But I wake each day to
Some strange dissipation.

I often forget simple
Words in our language,
That drive to distraction
And cause me more anguish,
But calm will return when
The evening is making
That brief interlude between
Sleeping and Waking.

Two to Choose

The sisters Newell were a shining jewel
That would pass my understanding,
We met at night when the moon was white
Out on the communal landing,
One was blonde, was a demi monde
The other brunette to the shoulder,
The legs of the blonde were lean and long
The brunette a little bit older.

I fell in love with them both at once
I think it was what they wanted,
For both, well versed in extravagance
Their ego's, each were undaunted,
The blonde would stalk in her Baby Doll
Next to her window, extended,
The other, naked, would read a book
Sprawling in view and bed-ended.

The blonde was the first to invite me in,
The other said she felt stranded,
We sat together like kith and kin
It's lucky that I am left handed,
They asked which one did I like the best,
I said, 'Now that would be telling.'
And kissed them both on the lips, to test
As the tears in their eyes were welling.

I had the choice, there were two to choose
The blonde had said she was willing,
The brunette said she was mine to lose,
I tossed for them with a shilling.

The blonde, I knew her as Flirty Anne
Picked heads, and lost in the tossing,
The other, I knew as Dirty Pam
Was out in the bathroom, flossing.

Death Plunge

We knew that the plane was going to crash,
We plunged through the air, on high,
We probably had five minutes to grieve
A minute to say goodbye,
She clung to me from her window seat
And cried, 'It's starting to fray.'
And through the port I could see the wing
As it tore, and twisted away.

'Why did you make me take this flight?'
She cried, as the others screamed,
'I could have been happily safe at home
If not for your stupid dream.'
She meant the holiday we had planned
Forever, to take in Rome,
The Coliseum, it still would stand
When they ferried our bodies home.

I felt quite peeved, for I didn't want
To take in those ancient piles,
But she'd insisted that Rome it was,
I wanted the Grecian Isles.
This wasn't the time for an argument
So I patted her crying cheek,
I needed to hear her 'I love you',
But that would have taken a week.

19

The plane was spinning, with just one wing
Was heading nose down to the ground,
And all the passengers screamed and cursed,
Stood up, were lurching around.
'Just get me my bag from the overhead,
It holds all our holiday cash,'
It didn't dawn on her she'd be dead,
To mention it would have been rash.

'At least we're together, Cheryl my love,'
I said, in calming her down.
We'd passed right through the cumulus cloud
So close we were to the ground.
The engine was screaming, the one we had
The emergency door flew wide,
And suddenly Cheryl was torn from her seat,
Sucked out of the aircraft, and died.

I sat in the blast from the open door,
My heart had stopped in my chest,
I cried, 'My God! Just let it be quick,
My lover has gone to her rest.'
'What lover's that?' said my Cheryl's voice,
From the foot of our bed, at home.
'You mean we're saved, that we have a choice?
There's no way we're going to Rome!'

The Christmas Gift

'It won't be much of a Christmas,'
I said to his woman, Kate,
As she met me in the garden,
And opened the garden gate,
I asked how well he was faring
And she answered, 'Not too well,'
Her eyes were blackened for lack of sleep
She looked like she'd been through hell.

While George lay out on a camper
Trying to get some air,
His lungs were riddled with cancer,
He said that he didn't care.
'I've had enough of this rotten life
It threw me a sucker punch,
I'll just be glad when it's over, mate,
Just think of me out to lunch.'

I couldn't say he'd get over it,
He'd catch me out in a lie,
The one thing both of us knew right then
Was George was about to die,
They'd given him just a week or so
Till his organs began to fail,
He might just make it to Christmas, but
That was the end of the tale.

But Kate was doing just what she could
To comfort his final days,
She'd come across to his neighbourhood,
When Kate decides, she stays,

They hadn't ever been love's young dream
Had parted the year before,
For George was always intolerable
Living with him was war.

And I would try to avert my eyes,
Whenever Kate was around,
I didn't want her to see me blush
So kept my eyes to the ground,
If only I had got to her first
I'd say to my mirror glass,
But far too late, she was with my mate,
He was way beneath her class.

And even though they had parted,
I couldn't begin to tell,
My feelings, how they were started
By being within her spell,
For she'd always been his woman,
Been his lover and his mate,
And even now they were parted,
I thought it a little late.

But he called me into the garden
To sit by his camper bed,
And said that he begged my pardon,
He knew he would soon be dead.
'But I have a gift to give you,
It might be a little late,
But at Christmas time I wish you
Would take care of my darling Kate.'

'I know that you care about her,
For I've seen you blushing and stare,
It's a year I've been without her,
Due to my lack of care,
But I think she'll come to love you,
You can ask yourself instead,'
For Kate was there in the garden,
And stood there, nodding her head.

The Devil's Crew

They 'pressed me on His Majesty's frigate
The H.M.S. Carew,
It only took me a day to find
I was lodged with the Devils's crew,
The Captain, 'Black Jack' Hawkins
Was a gentleman by name,
But on the ship he used the whip
To his undying shame.

I slipped and fell from the foremast arm
When I caught my foot in a stay,
And though a net kept me safe from harm
That wasn't the Captain's way,
He said I'd swim for my mortal sin
Told the crew to rope me through,
Then dragged me over the side and said,
'We're going to keel-haul you.'

The barnacles on the Carew's hull
Nearly tore my back to shreds,
My lungs were so close to bursting that
I thought that I was dead.

They hauled me over the side again
The deck was red from my back,
At least I knew I was safe again
From a sudden shark attack.

They rubbed raw salt in my many wounds
Till I thought I was in hell,
While some of the crew had mocked and jeered
The Devil's own cartel,
They wore tattoos of the skull and bones
It was strange for a Royal crew,
But they themselves had been Impressed
So they hated Hawkins too.

He used to stand on the quarter-deck
Quite close to the starboard rail,
Where he could see any slacking off
While we were under sail,
He'd tie the men to the nearest mast
And would whip, before the crew,
Till every man was inflamed and raw
And would plot what they would do.

It fell to me to devise a plan
That everyone agreed,
We had to get rid of this Devil man
It became our only creed,
So I took a rope when I climbed the mast
That was fixed above his head,
Then swung and booted him over the rail
So we thought that he was dead.

The crew then dashed to the starboard side
And they all looked down and cursed,
For Hawkins floated upon the tide,`
It couldn't be much worse,
He shouted up, 'This is mutiny!
I'll flay that man to the bone.'
But all he got were the jeers of the crew
As the Captain sank like a stone.

Just for Christmas

'It's only for over Christmas,' said
The son to his father there,
And watched as the old man's shoulders hunched
As he painfully mounted the stair,
'It's just for the festive season while
The house will be full of kin,
We're going to need your bedroom if
We're going to fit them in.

'I'll pick you up when the New Year dawns,
My promise is set in stone,
On the first or second of January
Expect me to bring you home.'
But the old man merely paused and turned,
The set of his mouth was grim,
'You don't need to make me promises,
I know I'm not wanted, Tim.'

And Tim would have said that wasn't true
But he had to heed his wife,
She'd said it was him or her would leave,
And her words cut like a knife,

'I'm always the one to wash and clean,
To cook, and pick up his mess,
He has to be gone by Christmas John,
I'll not put up with less.'

So early the morning of Christmas Eve
The son had packed a case,
And helped his father into the car
To head for the old folks place,
'It's lucky your mother's dead, my son,
You'd tear us both apart,
How do you think your Mum would feel,
I think you'd break her heart.'

And tears had run down the father's cheek,
And also down the son's,
Tim said, 'Look Dad, I am sorry but
There's nothing to be done.
I've said I'm coming to pick you up
So what more can I say?'
'I thought to be spending my Christmas
With my son, on Christmas Day.'

The car pulled up at the iron gate
And the son had forced a smile,
'It won't be long and with Christmas gone
It will just be a little while,'
He carried his case inside for him
And he turned to say goodbye,
When muttering 'Merry Christmas, Dad,'
The old man answered 'Why?'

The Demon Fish

I'd taken my friends way off the shore
In my small, glass-bottomed boat,
The weather was clear, the sea was calm
For the sturdiest boat afloat,
I wanted to scan the hidden depths
Watch all that lived on the reef,
But Peter my friend, just wanted to fish,
And so did his brother, Keith.

They busied themselves with their fishing rods,
Were bent on baiting their hooks,
When suddenly something beneath the boat
Made me take a second look,
It only appeared a shadow at first
Came on with a sinuous glide,
It wasn't a fish I had seen before,
'Hey, just look at this,' I cried.

They both turned around and peered below
But then the shadow had gone,
'What did you see,' said Peter P.
'It must have been twenty feet long!'
'Oh rubbish,' said Keith, 'beyond belief,
There isn't a fish of that size,
Not even the great White Pointer Shark,
You must have mud in your eyes.'

'I know what I saw,' I said again,
'It had the most horrible teeth,
It seemed to be looking for prey down there
Across the top of the reef.'

'I've fished these waters for twenty years,
I think I'd have seen it by now,'
Said Peter P. with a smirk at me,
'Watch us, and we'll show you how.'

They knew I wasn't a fisherman,
I wouldn't know Cod from a shark,
I just liked to watch the fishes swim
Through the glass-bottomed boat in the dark,
I'd rigged up floodlights to light below
That eerie, mysterious deep,
Where seaweed swayed in the land they played
With the rest of the world asleep.

The guys continued and cast their lines,
While I sat reading a book,
We'd be there hours, and that was fine
I took the occasional look,
We drifted over a patch of blue
The sand was clear below,
When back there came that sinuous shape
I said to the guys, 'HeLLO!'

This time it headed up for the boat,
Less like a fish than a snake,
A massive head with reptilian teeth
And suddenly I was awake.
It shot straight up, right over the boat
Snapping its massive jaw,
And took Keith's arm from his shoulder blades
Right into its mighty maw.

We just couldn't stop the flow of blood
It filled the boat as he died,
And Peter P. was distraught as he
Sat helplessly, and he cried.
'That must be some prehistoric beast
That lived on the ocean floor,
I'll never go fishing again,' said he
As we headed back to the shore.

Mary Anne

What shall I do with you, Mary Anne,
You went outside in the storming,
The lightning flashed and it struck you dumb,
You couldn't get up this morning.
I tried to give you a sweet caress
But you discharged on my finger,
I fear your voltage grows more, not less,
There's no good reason to linger.

I wrapped a cable around your toe
Ran it to earth in the garden,
Your toe as well as the cable glowed,
I'm sorry, I beg your pardon.
There's lightning flashes behind your eyes,
Your tongue is all of a sizzle,
The storm has gone but the rain keeps on
Although it's only a drizzle.

I took you out to our rubbish bin
The neighbours thought I was fooling,
And sat you down on the surface tin,
I thought that it would be cooling.

But soon the bin was a glowing red
I hauled you off from the garbage,
As flames and smoke took the garden shed
And put an end to our garage.

I thought that I'd better hose you down
When water hit, it was frightening,
The bolt ran over the garden hedge
And burnt it down with its lightning.
What shall I do with you, Mary Anne,
You know that I love you dearly,
But I'll never sleep in our bed again,
Till you are discharged, and feely.

The Adventure

She said she'd only be gone for a week,
I saw her off in the car,
'It's not that long,' she began to speak,
'It's not that I'm going far,'
So I waved goodbye and I turned to go,
I wish I could live it again,
For that was the last I saw of Flo
I'm missing her so, Amen.

Her mother phoned on the following day,
'What have you done with Flo?
She said we'd meet in the market place,
Did she even set out to go?'
I said she had on the previous day,
'Is she really not there?' I said,
And then my mind kept racing away,
I thought that she might be dead.

I called the police and the hospital,
And even the Fire Brigade,
No-one had ever heard of her
Or knew where she might have stayed,
Then I saw a clip on the news that night
She was walking along in the rain,
They were filming down at the station as
She was boarding the Melbourne train.

A week went by and I heard no more,
I thought that she might have phoned,
I saw her brother and sister too,
'I think that she's left,' I moaned.
'They hadn't heard, not a single word,
Since that man in an overcoat
Had called in, said he was looking for her,
And left her a simple note.

'Catch the plane at Tullamarine,
I'll meet you in Istanbul,
Pick up the pack from the man in green,
Make sure that the pack is full.'
'I thought you were going on holiday,'
Her brother had said to my face,
I said I didn't know where she was
She'd gone, with never a trace.

The bomb in the old Ramada Hotel
Went off, I saw on the news
The old city part of Istanbul,
They published a set of views,
And Flo was running from smoke and flames,
I saw her, clear as a bell,
And right behind was a man in green
In front of the old hotel.

They said a woman with auburn hair
Had dropped a pack at the desk,
And then had run, she carried a gun,
Was currently under arrest.
The following day, she got away,
Squeezed out through the window bars,
Then jumped in a waiting limousine,
One of the Russian cars.

I heard she went to Saint Petersburg,
Had asked for asylum there,
They'd said, 'No way,' that she couldn't stay,
She replied, 'It isn't fair!'
Nobody wanted to charge her so
They flew her on out to Wales,
And that's when I met her in Cardiff
Where we sat, with a couple of ales.

She said she had won an adventure
All hush hush, in an online quiz,
But had to deliver a package first,
'I should have asked what it is.'
She said she was sorry not telling me,
I reached out and held her hand,
'Where did you think you were going then?'
She said, 'to Disneyland!'

Witching Kate

Whenever I went with winsome Kate
She'd say, 'I'm a witch, and that,'
And while in bed, with love in my head,
All she would do was chat.
She'd chatter about the latest spell
She'd found in her old Grimoire,
While I would lie, and dream of her thighs
And hope she'd surprise me there.

And so she did, a number of times
Each time that I'd reach for her,
Like shifting sand, I'd find in my hand
A handful of pussy fur,
The black cat under the counterpane
Would wriggle and spit and scratch,
And I'd withdraw, away from its paw
I'd find it more than a match.

Then she'd go on about frogs and spawn
While up above in her flat,
And hanging down from her ceiling fan
The nastiest looking bat.
'I hope that's not going to drop on us,'
I'd say, but she didn't care,
It often lay on her pillow case
All tangled up in her hair.

'Wouldn't you like to make witching love?'
I'd say to her, in despair,
While she would lie, with spells in her eye
And some that would really scare.

33

She said she needed to concentrate
And would make some terrible moans,
They seemed to come from the mantlepiece
Where she kept a pile of bones.

She called them Fred, he was certainly dead
And he stared at us from above,
She'd cry, and say that there was a day
When he was her one true love.
But he'd fallen into her pickle jar
One day, when casting a spell,
And she'd pulled him out, too late, no doubt,
He'd pickled his way to hell.

I bid farewell to my witching one
Before I suffered his fate,
I'd prayed for love to heaven above
Knowing it was too late.
She'd filled a cauldron with toads and newts
Then turned and reached for my hand,
But I had fled, the moment she said,
'Now all I need is a man!'

The Caravan at Coffin Cove

I said, 'We're going to Coffin Cove
For the first weekend in June,
I've booked us a seaside caravan,
Under a bloodshot Moon,'
Giselda turned for a moment then
And she looked at me, wide-eyed,
'I've just come out of the hospital,
You know that I nearly died!'

'Why would you pick on Coffin Cove,
Isn't that testing fate?'
'That figure of death is out of breath,
He got to your bed too late.'
She'd had a terrible accident
And they thought she'd not survive,
But for a scar and the wreck of a car,
Here she was back, alive.

Giselda believed in portents and fate,
And something about the stars,
I said whatever the portents were,
She'd been driving the car.
'We hold our fate in our own two hands,
And yours just slipped on the wheel,
But though you bled, that scar on your head
Has just taken time to heal.'

So off we travelled to Coffin Cove
On the long weekend in June,
The caravan sat there on the sand
While the skies were dark with gloom.

35

We'd heard a storm was heading our way
Though we'd both be snug inside,
The beach was clear for the time of year
So Giselda swam, and dried.

The wind came up as the clouds rolled in
So we shut and locked the door,
With lightning crackling overhead
She huddled up on the floor,
She hated thunder, and lightning too
Then it rained, and turned to hail,
The noise was deafening there inside
Then the wind began to wail.

The van would rock as the wind would gust
So I held Giselda tight,
The storm just wouldn't let up, it raged
And roared all through the night,
We could hear the sound of the crashing waves
And they seemed outside our door,
Then the van took off, we could tell as much
By the movement of the floor.

I opened one of the windows just
To take a look outside,
Giselda said, 'Are we floating off?'
And I must admit, I lied.
The breakers crashed in a sea of foam
And we seemed far from the shore,
I said, 'Don't worry, this van is tough,
It could float for evermore.'

As midnight struck on my mantle clock
Giselda jumped, fell back,
'Who's that,' she pointed along the van
To a shape, all dressed in black,
Its hood half covered a grinning skull
And it held a wicked scythe,
Then in a rattling gravel voice,
'You'll not long be alive!'

I couldn't speak for a moment there,
The sight just took my breath,
I said, 'Just what do you want with us?'
'I'm here to bring you death!
I reign supreme over Coffin Cove
As you should have known full well,
I waited, knowing you'd wander in
To the seventh circle of Hell!

The van was tumbling in the waves
And turning round and round,
'I won't be using my scythe today,
The two of you will drown.'
But then a thunderous, monster wave
Threw me down on the floor,
And underneath us was solid ground,
We'd landed back on the shore.

The evil figure rose up at that
And turned to a greying mist,
Then suddenly he had gone complete
As she and I had kissed,
We burst on out through the open door
And we cried, 'We're still alive!'
'Don't ever bring me to Coffin Cove,'
Giselda said, 'Just drive.'

The Attic Room

My sister Susan had disappeared
At the age of twenty four,
She'd gone on up to the attic room
And she'd locked and barred the door,
We beat, cajoled, and entreated her,
But she never would come out,
I said, 'We shouldn't have argued Sue,
I didn't need to shout.'

My father came with his gravel voice
And demanded 'Open up!'
He thumped and kicked on the cedar door,
And beat with a metal cup,
But there wasn't even a whimper
As of somebody inside,
It was like she'd suffered a broken heart
Had crawled in there, and died.

We left her there till the morning,
Thought a night would calm her down,
'She'll come out once she is hungry,'
Said my brother, (he's a clown).
But as the clock struck for dinner time
With not the slightest stir,
My father carried a battering ram
And ran right up the stair.

He stood and battered the cedar door,
He said it gave him pain,
'I can't afford to replace it, but,'
Then belted it again,

The door had splintered, the lock fell off
And he burst into the room,
But all that he saw were cobwebs, dust
And an air of deepest gloom.

'Susan, where can you be,' he cried,
'There's nowhere you can hide,
There isn't even a window here
So you can't have got outside,'
His voice rang out through the house and sent
An echo down the stair,
My mother burst into tears to hear
That Susan wasn't there.

The police came over and climbed the roof,
Dropped into the attic space,
They hunted among the rafters there,
Looked almost every place,
There wasn't a sign of Susan though
She'd simply disappeared,
'The same thing happened to Grandma Coe,'
My mother cried, 'It's weird!'

'She locked herself in the attic there
In the fall of forty-eight,
'They thought that they heard her on the stair
When the hour was getting late,
But never a sign of her came back,
Then her husband, Grandpa died,
We always thought that she must be here
But somehow locked inside.'

We called the local clairvoyant in
And he brought his Tarot pack,
He stared long into his crystal ball
Till we had to call him back,
He chanted into the midnight hour
In a voice both loud and slow,
Till shuffling out of the Attic came
Not Sue, but Grandma Coe!

Reverse Spin

The sun went down on a Sunday night
And didn't come up again,
The clouds above were crimson and bright
And they shed life-giving rain,
The news came on at seven o'clock
In the morning, in the dark,
And said, 'No sign of the morning sun,
The view from here is stark.'

I bounded up and got out of bed
And I hit the ceiling fan,
My arms and legs and my head were light
So I turned about and ran,
With every step, when I floated up,
I hit my head on the door,
And when I tried to jump, I hovered,
Six feet off the floor.

The news came on for a second time,
A comet had hit the earth,
And halted the rotation of
The planet that gave us birth,

It seemed that one side would overheat
And the people there would roast,
While we would freeze on the dark side,
When the sea iced at the coast.

The temperature dropped down through the floor
And it soon began to snow,
The wife lay huddling up, and said:
'Now where are we going to go?'
But then the news had come through again
That a second comet hit,
Deep in the Russian tundra, and
The ground had shook with it.

It seems the earth had begun to turn
Once more, from the aftershock,
With everything back to normal then,
Whether it would or not,
But when the sun had come up again
We saw it rise in the west,
The week is reversed from Saturday,
What will they think of next?

The Witch of the Morning

There once was a wicked Warlock
Who lived on Crabtree Hill,
He lured the Witch of the Morning there
Who was my mother still,
My father, he was the patient type
Said, 'Son, she's just a witch,
And she'll be back in the morning, once
That Warlock's scratched her itch.

I didn't know what he meant just then,
I was far too young to know,
What people did in the darkness once
Their feelings overflowed,
But I was forever curious
And suppose that I am still,
I wanted to know, so had to go
On a trek up Crabtree Hill.

The Warlock lived in a copse of trees
In a tiny little shack,
A goat's head hung up above his door
I remember, looking back,
A window covered in mud and dust
Was the way I looked inside,
To see my mother down on her knees
Like a nasty Warlock bride.

I knew that I shouldn't be looking
Then she turned, and saw my face,
And stopped just what she was doing
Though I'd seen her loss of grace,

42

I turned to run, then I heard his voice
As he called my mother, 'Cath!'
Then caught me running off through the trees
As he stood, and blocked my path.

The man was a massive mountain,
And he wore a hat with horns,
His arms like a pair of Christmas hams
As he called, 'This one of yours?'
I fought and struggled and kicked like mad
As he took me into his shack,
While ever the Witch of the Morning smiled
And said, 'He's just my Jack.'

'I think we should cook him up for tea,'
Said the Warlock, with a wink,
And Cath, my mother said, 'Let me see,
I must have a little think.
I hope that he didn't see the act
Of love that I did for you,'
Then took my hand and opened the door
And motioned me out, said, 'Shoo.'

Now I'm a man, and I think on back
To that day on Crabtree Hill,
And just like the Warlock, I will stand
In front of my darling Jill,
While she gets down on her knees for me
On the floor, without a stitch,
To show me the love she has for me,
Just like the Morning Witch.

The Rose

We'd been together so long, it seemed
That nothing could tear us apart,
We lived our lives in a world of dreams
And Barbara lived in my heart,
But frost had covered the window pane
And then it began to snow,
As Barbara turned, with a look of pain
And said, 'It's best that you go.'

I didn't know what she meant at first
As I looked up from my book,
"Go where?' I questioned, but thought again
As she quelled my heart with a look.
'I said I want you to leave,' she cried,
And her face was set in stone,
'We've come to the end of the path,' she sighed,
'I want to be left alone.'

Then suddenly all confusion reined
I didn't know what to say,
Whatever had brought this mood on her,
I wished it would go away.
But she was firm, and she packed my things
And ushered me out the door,
I stood there shivering in the cold
To be back on my own once more.

I found a flat and I camped the night
There was barely a stick or chair,
I'd have to buy all the furniture
To make it a home in there.

But I sat and cried in the empty room
As the question came back, 'Why?'
I'd loved her so and my heart was torn,
I thought I wanted to die.

I went to her with my questions, but
She slammed the door in my face,
Whatever love she had had for me
Had vanished, without a trace.
It hurt so much that she cut me off
With never so much as a sigh,
I called that all that I wanted was
To tell me the reason, why?

The roses had bloomed so late that year
Were still in the garden bed,
We'd always tended the bush with joy,
We both loved the colour red,
So I snipped one off as I left one day,
And planted it under her door,
To let her know that I loved her still
I didn't know how to say more.

Her brother called in a week or so,
Said she was in hospital,
She'd gone in just for a minor cure
And thought that he'd better tell.
So I caught the bus and I went on down
With a quaking fear in my heart,
She hadn't said there was something wrong
Before she tore us apart.

The doctor came in his long white coat,
His brow and his face was grim,
I said, 'Don't tell me the news is bad,'
He said, 'I'm out on a limb.
Your wife just passed from the surgery,
But she pulled, from under her clothes,
And asked if I'd pass this on to you,'
In his hand was a red, red rose.

The Carnival Enterprise

I got a job at the Carnival,
All the fun of the fair,
With its Carousels and its Wishing Wells
And The Ferris wheel up there,
With a Gyro Tower and a Gravitron
You could hear the squeals of glee,
As they whirled about, and one fell out,
Nothing to do with me!

My only job was to strap them in
And I went from ride to ride,
They told me to familiarise
Myself with every side,
I loved the whirling Octopus
And the Swinging Pirate Ship,
But of them all, the Matterhorn
Was the one I found most hip.

I ended up on the Enterprise
At the closing of the night,
'Just two more rides,' the man announced,
'For a journey into fright!'

I strapped them into each Gondola
As the twenty patrons paid,
And heard their screams as they soared aloft,
I could tell they were dismayed.

The ride came down with a grinding halt
And I went to let them out,
But no-one sat in the Gondola's
Then I heard the Barker shout,
'Last ride, last ride in the Enterprise,'
And the twenty folk got in,
I said, 'What happened to all the rest?'
But he cried, 'Don't fuss now, Tim.'

The Enterprise had begun to spin
And carry them all aloft,
Then disengaged from its base and floated
Over a farmer's croft,
The sky was an inky black that night
And dotted with glittering stars,
And I swear today, I heard him say:
'They're heading on up to Mars!'

The Schoolyard Flirt

Marion Carrion, she was a tease,
She really knew how to flirt,
Would shake her hips and her moving bits
That were hidden under her skirt.
She'd beckon me out to the hockey field
And raise her skirt to the knees,
Said I could look at her secret nook
For only a simple 'Please.'

She had all a woman's mysteries
Although she was only a girl,
And knew the power of her nether bits
Would put my mind in a whirl.
So she showed her thighs with her flashing eyes
And then would have shown me more,
While I would share with a candid air
That I knew what she had in store.

Out there on the side of the hockey field
In the shade of the only bush,
We'd hide behind, so my hand could find
Whatever would make her flush.
I thought that I was the favoured one
While playing about with her toys,
But then I found on the soccer ground
She was sharing with all of the boys.

That moment of disillusionment
I thought would have broken my heart,
But I was tough and had seen enough,
There were other girls in the park.
So I thank Marion Carrion now
For her retrospect revelation,
She taught me well on the road to hell
And saw to my education.

The House the Cleric Built

We lived in a house a cleric built
In fifteen sixty-three,
Deep in a copse of Roman Elms
A grand and mighty tree,
The place was Tudor, half timbered,
And it creaked in every storm,
The wind was rattling through the eaves
Before we both were born.

We saw it up in the window of
The Realtor, going cheap,
It needed some TLC because
Its look would make you weep,
It badly needed a paint job and
Some timbers plugged with tar,
The years of rot had disfigured it,
'Are you interested?' 'We are!'

Dead leaves had cluttered the downstairs rooms
And damp had swelled the floor,
The leadlight windows were dark with gloom
There were rats down in the store,
We worked and slaved on it, Jill and I,
Till it soon became a home,
Nestling in a hollow that
The locals called a combe.

I'd lie awake in the poster bed
That had been since Cromwell's day,
The beams and curtains were overhead
And the wind would make them sway,

While Jill slept soundly, I still could hear
The wind sough through the trees,
Come rattling up to the shutters and
Slip gently past the eaves.

But then some nights, I'd hear some muttering
Down there by the elms,
Like ghosts of soldiers, loud and stuttering
Underneath their helms,
And then I'd hear the sound of marching
To a Roman beat,
There wasn't even a pavement but
It sounded like a street.

A street that clattered with cobblestones
To the sound of chariot wheels,
I'd stare on out from the window-sill
To see what night reveals,
But nothing moved in the shady wood
To make those strangest sounds,
I searched and searched in the daylight, through
Those ancient wooded grounds.

Then one day digging a garden patch
I came across a stone,
That held a funny inscription on
The face, that smacked of Rome,
I think it mentioned a Lucius
From Legion Twenty-Nine,
I pried it out of the ground and then
I knew what I would find.

He lay there still in his breastplate
With his helmet and his sword,
His sandals still on his feet and tied
On tight, with a rotted cord,
The skull stared up at me in dismay
As if to say, 'Who's there?
You've broken into my endless sleep,
Invaded my despair.'

I swiftly covered him over so
That Jill would never see,
A sight to give her the nightmares that
I knew would come to me,
But then I settled his stone upright
That he might rest in bliss,
And that was the end of the mutterings,
From that day until this.

Unrequited

She wasn't a striking beauty, but
I loved her with all my heart,
I know that I always meant to tell,
I should have done from the start,
But her presence had overwhelmed me
Every time that I saw her face,
I was far too shy as she passed me by
For she moved with a gliding grace.

She wasn't a social butterfly
But was always circumspect,
Was rather solemn and thoughtful but
Was all that I liked, direct.

I doubt if she even noticed me
Beyond becoming her friend,
I'd hoped for more, but I wasn't sure
It would turn out in the end.

And then a man had moved in next door,
With the moniker Richard Pace,
He had all the bling, was covered in rings
With assets all over the place.
He drove a mauve Lamborghini that
Spoke volumes about the man,
And it wasn't too long, he seemed to belong
For Esther was holding his hand.

I withered, retreated inside myself,
Retracted back in my shell,
My hopes and dreams, and my forward schemes
Were lost, and my heart as well,
I watched them drive in that magic car
While knowing that all was lost,
For all I had was a beat up Ford
At a fraction of the cost.

They say that money's not everything
But it's sure much better than none,
There wasn't much I was offering
But a heart, quite overcome.
I went for a while then I wandered out
While Esther was there on her own,
'Where have you been, I haven't seen you,
Have you been there on your own?'

I managed to mutter, my eyes cast down,
'I've watched you all over the place,
You seem to be settled, and riding round
With your new friend, Richard Pace.'
'Oh, him,' she chuckled, 'Old Diamond Rick,
He's full of himself for sure,
He thinks he's a gift to the ladies, but,
Me, I'm looking for more.'

My heart beat once, and it came to life,
I saw the spark in her eye,
'Now here's your chance,' said a tiny voice,
'All you can do is try.'
But my tongue was tied in its usual way
I never could blurt it out,
Then Esther said, 'I wish it were you,
You love me I know, no doubt!'

The Castle Bleak

The Queen had paid the eunuchs to
Decapitate the King,
And once the deed was done, she thought,
'I'm Queen of everything.'
She taxed the peasants to the hilt
Took half of every crop,
Her greed was quite rapacious, so
She never thought to stop.

She reigned up in the Castle Bleak
A fortress tall and grim,
That many armies tried to breach
But never could get in,

The only weakness she could see
From top, and looking down,
The trees that grew so tall against
The wall had made her frown.

'We'll have to chop those poplar trees
They're getting rather tall,
An army might climb up one night,
They're right against the wall,'
Her lover, Lord Chantrell had sighed
And tried to put her off,
'Those poplar trees are beautiful,
Too beautiful to chop.'

She didn't raise the point again
But went off to the tower,
Where she had locked the eunuchs to
Prevent them taking power,
She sent her German swordsman in
To do the deed, she said,
'I want to see you come on out
With every eunuch's head.'

The Queen was grim and merciless,
She'd act on every whim,
Her thoughts were dark and tortuous
And even with her kin,
Her cousin liked the mead too much
And slutted round the town,
Was gifted with a barrel of it,
Upside down, to drown.

She even chided Lord Chantrell
For eyeing off her maid,
She said, 'You two can go to hell,'
She thought the girl was laid.
They built a bonfire in the court
The maid was bound and tied,
And Chantrell watched the flames devour
The beauty he had spied.

One day upon the tower top
Chantrell unsheathed his blade,
And sliced his lover's head clean off
In payment for the maid,
Her head flew down the tower wall,
Her final thoughts were these:
'These branches break my fall, I'm glad
I didn't chop the trees.'

The Ending

The wind grew chill on a summer's day
And the clouds built up outside,
'It looks like a storm is coming our way,'
Said the folk of Ezra's Pride,
The sea rose up in a mighty swirl
And it swamped their coastal town,
'I think there's something wrong with the world,'
Said the blacksmith, Helmut Brown.

He left the forge as the fire went out
Under the tidal surge,
And looked to heaven as folk would shout
'The sea and the sky have merged.'

For the clouds above were purple and gold
The horizon coloured the same,
The ground beneath had rumbled and groaned
As it came, the pelting rain.

He went to look for his Isabelle
In the cottage down by the shore,
The water there was draining away
Then it hit the eaves once more,
And she clung onto the cottage roof
Where it swept her there in fright,
She cried to Helmut, 'Just get me down,
I fear for my life tonight.'

So he took her down in his brawny arms
And he waded through the flood,
'I'll keep you safe from the world's alarms,'
As he walked through seas of mud,
He walked her up to the higher ground
As the lightning lit the sky,
'I'll not let anything happen to you
For in truth, I'd rather die.'

But then the ground had opened up
In a crevice, ten feet deep,
And he was parted from Isabelle,
Who stood on the side more steep,
'How can I come on back to you,'
The love of his life had cried,
As he stood still as the crevice grew
So wide, on the other side.

'The world is trying to tell us things,
It's tearing us all apart,

Perhaps we haven't been kind to it,
It's punishing us, sweetheart.'
And she had moaned, his Isabelle,
Stood out in the pouring rain,
'Well what have I ever done to it?
The planet is going insane.'

Then the thunder growled up overhead,
As if to refute a lie,
'It's you who are insane,' it said,
'Get ready to say goodbye.'
And a lava flow came down the hill
In a stream, and glowing red,
'Don't let it come near you, Isabelle,
Just a touch, and you'll be dead.'

We'll leave them there on that distant hill
Where the world keeps them apart,
'Why should you be untouched,' it said,
'When you folk have broken my heart.
You have drilled through me, and spilled on me,
And have fouled my lakes and seas,
Why should I leave your perfect love
When I'm filled with your disease?'

The Green Room

We'd picked up the cottage for peanuts, as
It sat on the edge of a wood,
The air was damp and we used a lamp,
No power in that neighbourhood,
But the sun came filtering in through the leaves
On the pleasant summer days,
It was like we were living a hundred years
In the past, using former ways.

We carried our water in from a well
That sat just outside the door,
We had to lower a wooden pail
And it slopped all over the floor,
But Meredith laughed, and said it was fun,
She felt like a pioneer,
'I'm getting to know how things were done
In the neck of the woods, round here.'

We fired the stove and the hearth with wood,
Gathered among the trees,
For branches fell, in the storms as well
When the wind was more than a breeze,
I chopped it up on a wooden block
And carted it all inside,
To see it stacked by the kitchen clock
Gave me a sense of pride.

Upstairs was a single bedroom with
An attic room beside,
The walls were covered with wallpaper
From a distant time and tide,

The bedroom was an ocean blue
And the attic was painted green,
I said to Meredith, 'Shield your eyes,
It's the brightest thing I've seen.'

The damp had got in the attic wall
And the paint had started to rot,
Up in one of the corners you
Could see a slight fungus spot,
But we didn't need the room just then
So I said, 'Just let it be.
I'll find the time to attend to it
When the rest has set me free.'

But Meredith's sister came to stay
So we had to use the room,
We turned it into a bedroom with
A flick of a whisking broom.
Rhiannon was a beauty, I'll
Admit that she took my breath,
So young, and with her life unsung
And yet she was close to death.

She'd been and slept in the Green Room
For a week, or maybe more,
When she said, 'I fell, and I feel unwell,'
Then she coughed up blood on the floor.
So Meredith was distraught, and thought
She'd sleep at her sister's side,
But early the following morning she
Then told me her sister died.

She stayed with her sister's body there,
She said it was like a tomb,

And soon my Meredith coughed up blood,
She said 'It's an evil room!'
A doctor came with the ambulance
And looked at the flaking mould,
Then said, 'I think it's the paint, my dear,
I've heard of this stuff of old.'

He scraped it then, and he tested it
And he came back round to see,
'You know that paint's full of arsenic,
There's a well known history.'
And life was never the same for us
When we sat in the cottage gloom,
I could always hear Rhiannon's cough
Up in that attic room.

While Meredith put the blame on me
Packed up her things and left,
She said that I should have scraped it off,
Then left me, feeling bereft,
She'd lost her sister, and I lost her
So I sit alone in the gloom,
My heart has stopped like a ticking clock,
And the cottage, now, is a tomb.

Cape Grace

The lighthouse at Le Cap de Grace
Was damp and dark at best,
The rain would sweep in from the south,
The wind rage from the west,
But nature's torments could not match
The storms that formed within,
For deep inside its battered walls
Were palls of mortal sin.

Two lighthouse keepers kept the light,
Both Jon and Jacques De Vaux,
They tended to the light above
While she would wait below,
The dusky, husky buxom witch
With lips of honey dew,
Who loved the lighthouse keepers,
Not just one, but even two.

Below was but a single bed,
She said that they must share,
They watched her eagerly each night
Her tend and brush her hair,
For then she would turn round to them
And indicate her choice,
She'd merely point at one of them,
Not even use her voice.

And then the chosen one would smile
His brother often curse,
For he would share her bed that night
The other fare much worse,

For he would lie inside the store
On coils of hempen rope,
And lie awake and listening,
No sound would give him hope.

But often she would cry aloud
In passion through the night,
While Jon or Jacques would stop his ears
And think, 'It's just not right.'
But she ruled this menage a trois
With silken hand and glove,
And they would never question it
While working up above.

She only ever favoured each
For just a single night,
She knew to show a favourite
Would seem to them like spite,
And thus the nightly balance kept
Their tempers both in check,
She fed on their desires, and they
In turn showed her respect.

The winter storms came in to stay,
The waves beat down below,
The wind beat at the lighthouse glass
And one would have to go,
Above to guard that precious light
To keep the ships from harm,
But who would go aloft would cause
The brothers both alarm.

For he who stayed would taste the charms
Of Elspeth for that night,
It might not be his turn, and that
They both thought wasn't right,
A rising tide of anger fed
By storms and mute dismay,
Turned brother against brother when
One had to go away.

One night the light went out, and Jon
Said, 'Jacques, go up above,
Your turn it is to light the light
While I stay with our love.'
But Jacques refused his brother's plea
And said, 'No, you can go,
You had the bed of love last night,
I'm staying down below.'

The night was dark and moonless and
There wasn't any light,
While out there in the darkness rode
A freighter in the night,
It drove up on the reef, its bow
Then battered in their door,
And pinned their husky, dusky witch
In blood pools on the floor.

The lighthouse at Le Cap de Grace
Is damp and dark at best,
The rain will sweep in from the south,
The wind rage from the west,
Two lighthouse keepers keep the light
And share the only bed,
The half love that they long for now
Is well and truly dead.

The Old Man's Muse

I sit in the room in my easy chair
And ponder my life in the gloom,
The source of my wonder is where did it go,
While racing me on to the tomb,
I thought that forever was all that I had
Before me, when barely a teen,
But now in my dotage I look back upon
The little that lay in-between.

It used to be easy when I was young
And supple and fit, without care,
I didn't believe it would come so undone
But that was when I was still there.
The aching of muscles and creaking of bones
Were something that old people had,
And I was determined to die, before moans
Would rack me, and make me feel bad.

But life is deceptive, it sneaks up on one,
By not even making a sound,
It pads up behind you before you can look
And then it starts beating you down.
We cling to our dreams and impossible schemes
And hope that our time will come in,
Just as the ship of our fortunes will stream
In to shore, with the laurels we'll win.

I never got married, or tied myself down
For why should I borrow a book?
With so many women abroad in the town
And each could be had, with a look.

So that was my folly, and that was my creed,
I bedded each one as they came,
I knew no regret as I scattered my seed,
Nor even the feeling of shame.

I heard people mention that love was the thing
But I didn't know what they meant,
Was love a new sports car, or masses of bling,
I carried that stuff on my belt.
My friendships were shallow, and selfish I know,
I look back, and measure the past,
If my life were a steamer, they'd take it in tow
And fly all my flags at half mast.

There once was a woman, I'll call her Karrel,
Who worked her way into my heart,
I almost felt things that I never could spell
And soon we had drifted apart.
But her presence had lingered so long in my mind
That I spent my days, just feeling sad,
She said I was empty, and heartless, unkind,
Till I thought I was quite going mad.

So now I sit here, quite alone in my chair
And I ponder on where it went wrong,
The tears on my cheeks tell me life was unfair
That it got the wrong words to my song.
But deep in the dark of my shrivelled old heart
Where Karrel still resides, fancy free,
I look in my shame for somebody to blame
And the answer comes back, it was me!

The Dancing Girl

I walked on down to the travelling show
Thinking to take a ride,
When the barker said, in a voice so low
'There's a Dancing Girl inside.'
He opened the flap of the crimson tent
And he tried to wave me in,
I said I didn't know what he meant,
He replied, 'What price for sin?'

I said I wanted to take a ride
Not look at a Dancing Girl,
There were plenty down at the local club
In my easy, sleazy world.
'There's not a thing she could teach me now
For I've seen it all before.'
He said, 'This girl is the Jezebel
Who performed for Kings, and more.'

I waved him off and I carried on
In my search for a thrilling ride,
And spent the evening whirling, twirling
Over the countryside,
But as I turned to travel on home
I passed by the crimson tent,
And the barker opened the flap again
To see if I would relent.

It must have been curiosity
For I turned and went inside,
Into its darkened depths I went
To flatter his wounded pride,

There was eastern music playing low
And I heard a woman wail,
Kneeling in front of an altar there
And the name inscribed was 'Baal.'

She heard me there, and got to her feet,
And danced like an ancient rhyme,
But underneath the paint on her face
Was the ravage of endless time,
Gold and silver glittered and gleamed
From the very little she wore,
With chains and bracelets jangling as
She danced around, like a whore.

She pressed her body against me then
And jabbered some foreign tongue,
The only word that I thought I heard
Was the one on the altar, One!
The barker stood in the entranceway
And she muttered his name, aloud,
She said Ahab, and I thought to run
He stood in the way, and bowed.

She pushed me up to the altar then
And tried to force me to kneel,
I thought of the Bible story, and
My skin had crawled at her feel,
I fought her off, and pushed her away
The man she called Ahab scowled,
And as I left by the flap of the tent
The dogs by the entrance howled.

The Cupboard

There once was a tiny cupboard, and
We kept our groceries there,
Just enough room for two to squeeze
Inside, and under the stair,
And Karen would beckon me go to her
With just an arch of her brow,
She wouldn't take no for an answer, but
Would say, 'Just come to me now.'

Then I would go in and close the door
And feel her close in the gloom,
Her skirt would rustle, I'd feel her thighs
And would smell her sweet perfume,
She had such a sense of urgency
When she pulled me down to her breast,
But I would be telling old secrets to
Reveal what's happening next.

But that was a million years ago,
It seemed the beginning of time,
When we were young, and I'd taste her tongue
Sweeter than strawberry wine,
Those nights were the nights of passion, but
Then nothing could really compare,
With the times when Karen called to me
To meet her under the stair.

But the years unfolded fatefully,
And Karen began to stray,
Her eyes that once had been more than wise
Would seem to have gone away,

She'd stare out into the distance to
Some place that I'd never been,
And when I'd ask her just where she went
She'd mutter, 'What do you mean?'

I found her wandering down the road
Just down from St. Michael's dome,
She looked at me, most piteously,
'I don't know how to get home.'
I took her hand and I led her back
Through the early morning frost,
And when we got to our gate, she said,
'Oh God, I seem to be lost.'

The days ahead were a nightmare, she'd
Forget where she'd put the pans,
Then look at me like a stranger, when
I'd reach out, and hold her hands,
But worst of all, she would bring my tears
When she stood by the cupboard stair,
And say, 'I seem to remember, but
Just what did we do in there?'

Poor Robin

The North Wind doth blow,
And we shall have snow,
And what will poor Robin do then,
Poor thing…

The house that poor young Robin bought,
You'd scarcely call it a house,
A single room on a farmer's farm
You'd not swing even a mouse.
But he moved on in, and tidied it up
And asked Rosemary to stay,
She sat in silence, her knees clamped tight,
And her first response, 'No way!'

'There isn't a cupboard to keep a broom,
The kitchen's there by the wall,
We couldn't live in this tiny room
To even think, I'm appalled.'
But Robin said, 'It's just for a start,
I'm going to build on a wing,
I'm making the bricks from mud and straw
It will all be done by the Spring.'

So Rosemary had unpacked her case,
And hung her clothes on a hook,
Then looked in vain for a tiny shelf,
There wasn't even a book.
But Robin slaved, out in the yard,
Making his bricks from straw,
The walls went up and the roof went on,
And he laid the wood for the floor.

At first they slept on the floor inside,
And Rosemary kept it clean,
She said, 'Don't touch, till I am a bride,'
And pillows went in between.
He put his love all into his wing,
All carpeted now, and swish,
And set it up as a bedroom then,
'Are you coming to bed?' 'You wish!'

She only ever kissed with a peck,
She never opened her lips,
He wanted more, but couldn't be sure,
As he nibbled her fingertips.
Then one day, down came the winter rain
And the wind it was blowing cold,
Rosemary lay there shivering so
She allowed him just one hold.

His hand had strayed, down where it would
You'll admit we'd do the same,
But he found down there, in that neighbourhood
Something that changed the game.
He leapt on up, and he washed his hands,
Said, 'You're not even a girl!'
'Didn't you guess,' said Rosemary,
'It's not the end of the world.'

She chased him all around in that room,
'I thought you wanted to play,'
While Robin stood, his back to the wall,
While holding her off, 'No way!'
He fled into his favourite wing,
And hammered and bolted the door,

His bricks were melting out in the rain
And mud flowed over the floor.

She went on back to the troupe 'Les Girls',
While Robin stayed on the farm,
You'll not see him venturing out these days
He lives in a state of alarm.
With just the sight of a petticoat
He's a shuddering, gibbering wreck,
And ask him if he will leave his wing,
The answer comes back, 'Like heck!'

He'll flee to his farm,
To keep him from harm,
And hide his head under his wing,
Poor thing!

The Black Bus

The bus rolled up, and parked on the green
It was painted black outside,
With just one sign, up over the door,
'Come in for a hell of a ride.'
So the neighbours gathered around the bus
And the wife went up to the door,
She said, 'Come on, stop making a fuss,
What are you waiting for?'

My Dawn has always been quick to jump
She'll do most things for a fling,
She gets herself in trouble enough
By trying most everything,

She once got stuck on the Ferris Wheel
When she got right up to the top,
Then the lights went out, and they all went home
And the seat began to rock.

You'd think that that would have cured her when
She spent the night in the air,
Freezing her butt in the darkness and
Tied to a swinging chair,
When the wind blew up and the rain came down
And the lights in the fair went out,
She swears that she almost lost her voice
For the times that she tried to shout.

Now here she was at the door of a bus
That was black, and dim inside,
You couldn't see through the tinted glass
I know, for we all had tried,
The neighbours stood there, egging her on
Though they stood well back in fear,
While Dawn rapped hard on the bus's door,
Nobody else went near.

The door slid back with an evil swish
And revealed a dim red glow,
She said 'Come on,' and I said 'You wish,'
She called me a so-and-so,
But climbed the step and the door slid shut
Locking us all outside,
The diesel roared as it started up,
Drove into the countryside.

That said it might have been Martians or
Some pinhead freaks from the Moon,

We didn't know what they came here for
But we all would find out soon,
I hate to think what they did to her
In the glow of that evil bus,
Or if there was only the driver, but
He sure wasn't one of us!

They found her out in a country lane
Or at least, what there was left,
I went quite crazy with grief, for I
Had never felt so bereft,
They'd taken her heart, and her kidneys, lungs
And even the balls of her eyes,
So now we knew what that sign had meant,
'Come in for a hell of a ride.'

If ever you see a big black bus
Roll up and park on the green,
Stay well away from the door, or pay
The price that my Dawn has seen,
It's there to collect the organs from
Unwary ones, and it steals
Whatever it can from mortal man,
It's really a hell on wheels!

Ghost

There's a new thing up on the Internet
And it's how some people 'Ghost',
They date and chat, but it's after that
That they disappear the most.
You think you're starting a new romance
And that they are full of you,
But they never say that they're gone today,
That they won't be back, it's true!

They once would call, and they'd ring the bell
And stand on the hallway mat,
Then face to face with a lack of grace
They would say 'That's the end of that!'
But that caused tears and was much too hard
For the one who'd want to leave,
When the jilted one said that's not much fun,
And cry on the leaver's sleeve.

Then the mobile phone came to everyone
And they all began to text,
It wasn't long before right or wrong
They would use that method next,
They'd text, 'Too bad, but I've changed my mind,
I can't take you to the ball,'
Then days would pass and you soon would find
Your romance had hit the wall.

But then at least you could text your Jack
And call him a piece of scum,
' You had to do it behind my back,
With a text, you cut and run.

You've not the guts of a greasy toad
For you couldn't face to face,
You didn't tell me in bed last night,
You're an absolute disgrace!'

So texting slowly went out of vogue
It was hard to change your Sim,
Every time that they'd text you back
So they'd think, 'He's never in.'
It's far more easy to slip away
Get lost in a cyber mist,
Block your love on your Facebook page
It's as if you don't exist.

You slip away like a silver wraith
With the substance of a fog,
Nevermore to be seen by them,
Of course, you're a dirty dog!
But that's the way of the Internet
If you come across a ghost,
Avoid the dating sites online
Or your love life will be toast.

The Premonition

There's something wrong, for I see it now
Burn brightly in my brain,
A simple spark and a flash of light
That becomes a roaring flame,
It happens just about every night
As I rest my weary head,
And burns my eyes from the insides, when
I'm lying still in bed.

The doctors say it's a trick of light
At the corner of my eyes,
Perhaps it's only a lightning flash
That catches, by surprise,
But there's no light in my darkened room
And the blinds are pulled down tight,
It comes so suddenly, then it goes
Like a spark of some insight.

Could it be something that's been and gone
Though I've blacked the memory out,
Something terrible, that went wrong
And scared me, without doubt?
Could it be something that's still to come
Said the gypsy in the hall,
While crossing her palm with silver, as
She peered in her crystal ball.

'It could be a warning from the gods,
It could be a sign of fate,
Some sort of a premonition that
You attended to, too late,

The crystal ball has a fiery glow
In its depths, that I never saw,
And many's the time I've gazed in it
Not seeing such glow before.'

I never would worry Christabel
With my tale of the nightly flame,
I wouldn't have wanted her to think
There was something wrong with my brain,
So she went and ordered her wedding dress
A vision in silk and lace,
And yards and yards of a satin trail
With net all over her face.

We took our vows in the Baptist church
She'd attended since a child,
Keeping her mother happy, though
In fact, she was meek and mild,
Then later at the reception we
Arrived at the old church hall,
And Christabel was a vision as
She stood by the entrance wall.

There's no way I could foresee it
Though I later thought that I should,
A guest came in with a cigarette,
I'd have stopped him if I could,
He flicked the butt and a single spark
Flew onto my darling's train,
The silk and satin went up at once
And Christabel was aflame.

The flames went up like a giant torch
And engulfed the yards of net,
There wasn't time for a single word
If there was, then I forget,
She stood there blackened, her skin peeled off
And she swayed against the wall,
Then slowly toppled to earth before
I reached, to stay her fall.

Now every night there's a single spark
And a sudden flash of light,
As flames are dancing behind my eyes
In that awful nightmare sight,
The tears that roll down my cheeks are hot
As if roasted in the fire,
They might as well, for I dwell in hell
Since I lost my one desire.

The Witch of Dreams

You didn't tell me, when I found you
That you were the Witch of Dreams,
You conjured spells in your afternoons
Of many and varied scenes.
When late at night put the sun to flight
And the moon rose over the hill,
You'd lie in bed, and you'd lay your head
In the dreams you are dreaming still.

You'd fill my head with colours and dread,
With your images light and dark,
And take my hand on a stretch of sand,
Or dance in a Faery Park,

79

I never knew if the scenes were you
Or spells, raised up in the mist,
With a goblin, elf, or your own sweet self,
And lips that I'd never kissed.

Your scenes float over the cyber seas
And come to rest in my head,
They take my words from a grim disease
That I may have written or read,
You conjure scenes that are lost in time
And you bring them back to my eyes,
Then I recall, with the tears that fall,
Each love, its time and demise.

Your dreams will ever bewitch me, girl,
Your scenes will tug at my heart,
Whatever spells are in store for me
You'll send, though we are apart.
We neither dwell in the real world
In truth, for we've never met,
But surely, you are the Witch of Dreams
As sure as your name's Jeanette.

*(for Jeanette Leone Skirvin, who has made
So many delightful videos of my early poems)*

Besotted

I've followed you out in the yard,
And then when you mounted the stair,
I thought I was watching an angel,
But you didn't know I was there.
You moved with such elegant grace,
That I couldn't help but stare,
You seemed so above and beyond me,
That all that I felt was despair.

We'd pass in the pit of the stairwell,
Your latté, you held in a cup,
When I'd see you coming toward me,
I'd hope, but you'd never look up.
My heart would rebound in my ribcage,
I'd turn and I'd stare at your back,
I wondered how I could approach you
And worked on a plan of attack.

Perhaps I could trip, and I'd stumble,
And push you right into the wall,
Then clutch at you, ever so humble,
And tell you that I was appalled.
At least I could get you to see me,
You couldn't ignore me again,
But when it came down to it, clearly,
An angel's beyond mortal men.

The love that I felt was like heartburn,
It plagued all my nights and my days,
I'd torture myself with each notion,
And plotted in various ways,

I constantly thought of your beauty,
And hardened myself to the task,
'I wondered,' I said, ' if you knew me?'
You sighed, 'I thought you'd never ask.'

Adrift

There were twenty women and fourteen men
From the wreck on that tiny spit,
Lost in that mighty ocean, just a
Mile was the most of it,
There were pigs galore from a previous crew
Who'd been wrecked some years before,
And plenty of veg, they fished from a ledge
Jutting out, and over the shore.

So in time the fourteen had paired them off
And it left, forlorn, the six,
There wasn't a single partner left
For the girls to scratch their itch,
So they huddled up and began to plot
How to thin out the ranks of those
Who took up the men that were meant for them,
They started by shedding their clothes.

There were naked breasts that they thought would test
The men in the rival camp,
Would lure them off in the undergrowth
To lie where the earth was damp,
And it worked for some, though the men returned
To the partners they chose before,
'The only way that they're going to stay,'
Said the six, 'is to go to war.'

Charmaine was found in a grove of trees
With her face, all covered in blood,
And Derek didn't seem too displeased
He latched onto Maxine Flood,
But the thirteen said, her blood was red,
And they looked askance at the five,
'We need to arm, and raise the alarm
If we're going to stay alive.'

But a dozen died in the camp that night,
The soup had given them cramps,
Eleven woman had taken flight
And the one old man, called Gramps,
That left a surplus of thirteen men
And the women numbered seven,
'There's not enough to go round,' they said,
But the women were in heaven.

The six bereft of the men were left
To mumble and scheme and plot,
'We need to kill at least six of them,
Whether we want, or not!'
So late at night in the pale moonlight
There were shadows abroad in the trees,
And before the dawn, the six had gone,
Beaten down to their knees.

There were six and six, you would think it fixed,
In a year they'd be in hell,
For two of the girls lay down, were nixed
Gave birth, in a winter spell,
The men denied said they had their pride
And attacked their mates of yore.
But somehow managed to kill all three,
So now there were three and four.

'We'll keep the fourth in reserve,' they said,
'In case of a sudden death,'
But Maxine Flood was in no such mood
Though she sat, and she held her breath,
They made her fish and they made her cook
While she worked upon her wish,
And when just one of the men was gone
She fed them puffer fish.

'Now there's only you, and there's only me,'
She called, when he wandered back,
Staggering into the camp, he said,
'I've been in a shark attack!'
His arm was missing, he bled right out,
And died in front of her eyes,
While Maxine Flood had rolled in his blood
And cried to the empty skies.

Time Was...

I stare at you and you stare at me,
That picture of me before,
You looked so young in your pedigree
Before we both went to war,
But life has left its mark on the face
That was captured, back in time,
And now there's little left of your grace,
There's nothing that's left of mine.

For you're a constant reminder of
The man that I thought was fine,
I look in awe at your forehead where
There isn't a single line,

Not one of the cracks and crevices
That now will litter my brow,
I wonder how you would feel, if you
Were able to see me now?

If only I had been painted like
The Picture of Dorian Gray,
Then you would possibly look like me
And I'd be like you today,
My faults and pleasures you'd never know
Except on your painted face,
And you would never be put on show,
While I would retain your grace.

But time and life are a cruel pair,
For age to them is a joke,
They both conspire to grey your hair
From the time you enter their yoke,
They run their tractors over your face
Emasculate skin and bone,
And when you look, there isn't a trace
Whatever you were, has flown.

No sweet young thing will look at you now,
If so, she's telling you lies,
The only sign of the love you've known
Will still reside in your eyes,
And so you look at your lady now
Who stuck by you, thick and thin,
And praise the Lord that she's aged like you,
As you're falling in love again.

Dark Spot

Erika loved her horse, Dark Spot,
The spot was between its eyes,
And everywhere Erika rode with it,
They said it was no surprise.
'That spot's right there on its forehead, girl,
It shimmers in rain and mist,
Before we see who the rider is
We see that mark, like a fist.'

And true, it looked like a fist, it did,
A fist all covered in blood.
The horse was black but the fist was red,
Red-brown, as if it was mud.
She loved that horse with her very life
And he must have loved her too,
That bold black galloping stallion did
Whatever she wanted to do.

But Saul de Vere was a jealous man,
And watched whenever she'd ride,
He had a passion for Erika's hand
And wished to make her his bride.
She wasn't ready to settle down
And said that he'd have to wait,
But every time she was saddling up
He'd stand by the stable gate.

'Why do you love that horse so much?'
His anger tended to flare,
'I'd give my all for a tender touch,
You act as if I'm not there!'

'When you can carry me on your back,
And gallop through hills and dales,
And make me feel like he makes me feel
With the wind, full blown in my sails...

Then maybe I'd take a look at you,
But you're still tied to the earth,
Better you had four legs that flew
And a mare had given you birth.'
Then Erika laughed, and wheeled about
And galloped off in the mist,
To leave him fume at her parting jest,
A man who'd never been kissed.

His anger soon got the best of him
And he loaded his scatter-gun,
He waited out in the woods for them,
Not give them the chance to run,
He'd blow a hole in that horse's chest
And bring it down to its knees,
Then put a shot in that horse's head,
Not listen to Erika's pleas.

The horse came galloping through the trees
The wind in Erika's hair,
She laughed and sang as she rode along
Then saw de Vere standing there.
She screamed out loud as he levelled the gun
And fired point blank at the horse,
It's blood sprayed out of its wounded chest
But still, it kept on its course.

The eyes of the stallion glowed bright red,
Its hooves bit deep in the turf,
Some demon took on the horse's soul
As it ran its killer to earth.
The last thing ever de Vere would see,
A spot that looked like a fist,
It cracked his skull as it ran him down
And buried him deep in the mist.

Now Erika has a fine young horse,
She brought him back from the stud,
She said it had a stallion sire
That had a spot on its head.
And never will she marry a man
She said, 'they're tied to the earth,
They're all the same in the human clan
When a mare's not given them birth.'

The Woman I Didn't Know

Elizabeth Paddington Warrington Ware
I met on a path today,
I knew by the wind that was blowing her hair
She'd not have a lot to say.
I said my hello and she turned then to go
And she stuck her nose up in the air,
Like she didn't know me, or sought then to throw me
Which I didn't think very fair.

I said, 'Aren't you talking?' but she just kept walking
So I turned around and caught up.
I caught at her sleeve in a moment of peeve
And in doing, spilt tea from my cup,
She snapped 'Understand me, young man, and unhand me
You're showing that you have no couth!'
I thought she was blind or was being unkind
I'm a pensioner, far from a youth.

'Don't say you don't know me, you're trying to snow me,
Remember, we once had a fling,'
I had her engaged, but she flew in a rage
And said, 'I don't recall such a thing!
You're merely a stranger, I feel I'm in danger,
I'm calling for help in a thrice,'
'How could you forget me, with all that you let me
Back then, don't you think it was nice?'

'I'm Ellen Pengellen O'Fogarty Fair,'
She exclaimed, and I said, 'then you're not...
Elizabeth Paddington Warrington Ware,
I'm so sorry, I must have forgot.'
I thought, 'I'm in trouble, she must have a double,'
Then thought of the tat on her bot,
'Do you have a sailor?' She blushed, I had nailed her,
For Fair she was certainly not!

The Devil's Mill

Down at the end of Kilmartin Street
Where nobody seems to go,
A widow lives in an ancient mill
Where the river will overflow,
The mill race turns the mighty wheel
Though it grinds no wheat or corn,
It's not been used as a working mill
Since before we both were born.

And the widow there is a mystery,
For we don't know where she's been,
She doesn't give out her history
Though we know her name's Christine,
She's rarely seen in the street outside
But the gown she wears is black,
And those that visit and go inside
Are rarely seen to come back.

And I've watched myself, that paddle wheel,
It seems to go in reverse,
Whenever she has a visitor there
It's as if the mill is cursed,
For then the water flows uphill
It's against all laws, I know,
Whoever heard of the water going
Back to the overflow?

There's a warning sign on the portico
And a warning sign within,
'Don't think to enter the Devil's Mill
If your life is filled with sin,

For it may get rid of the things you want
And delete the good things too,
You may uncover a life within,
But of course, that's up to you.'

I went one day to the portico
And beat on the old front door,
Then heard her footsteps begin to echo
Across the flagstone floor,
The door flung wide and she stood aside
And I walked into the mill,
But heard the grind of the wheel rewind
Outside, I can hear it still.

I felt my head beginning to spin
As I travelled back in time,
Undoing every single action
That once I'd thought were mine,
Then once outside, I stood and cried
For my world was not the same,
I'd lost my only love, my bride
And forgotten our baby's name.

I thought I'd possibly get them back
If I went again to the mill,
And stood just cautiously inside
While the wheel went forward still,
But the widow blocked the door to me
And she said, 'Don't come again,
You only get but a single chance
Or the end result is pain.'

The Poseur

She was always saying she'd kill me,
Was violent in word and in act,
But a heart of gold, so her friends have told,
They say it as if it's a fact.
But they'd never had to live with her,
And often, I think it's true,
That you only know what's in somebody's soul
Whenever you have, or you do.

They thought her the life of the party,
All giggles and kicking up heels,
When we were alone, she'd curse and she'd moan,
Just ask me, I know how it feels.
She'd slander each friendship behind their back,
While they were left thinking it fine,
I didn't care much for the friends she'd attack,
But then she'd get stuck into mine.

They'd not see her tempers and tantrums,
Weren't there with her stamping her feet.
I'd heard it said she was good in bed,
She'd wrap herself up in a sheet.
She gave out that she was broadminded
Would flash both her cleavage and thighs,
But never at home, when we were alone,
She'd do it for all other guys.

I never could do a thing right for her
She held me in bitter contempt,
While I'd try to raise her, to lift and to praise her,
She'd just say that I was unkempt.

I took her one day for a picnic lunch,
We sat at the top of a cliff,
The weather was balmy, I thought it would calm me,
It did, but her manner was stiff.

She soon resurrected an argument
I thought that was over and done,
My mind was quite hazy, but she was stone crazy,
And soon she had started to run.
I stood at the edge of the towering cliff
With her charging at me, and how!
She came in a rush, but she missed in her push
Or I wouldn't be writing this now.

The Cave

I'd known of the cave beneath the cliff
For a year, or maybe more,
And I'd often said to Jill, 'What if...'
But we'd not been there before.
It was only at the lowest tide
That the entrance could be seen,
We'd have to dive, to swim inside
And for that, Jill wasn't keen.

For the cave lay in a tiny cove
With towering cliffs above,
'So how are we going to get down there,
To swim,' said Jill, 'my love,'
We'll hire a boat and we'll cruise around
With our gear, from Canning Bay,
Which is what we did with our scuba tanks
On a fresh, mid-winter day.

It took a couple of hours or more
To get to the favoured spot,
The sea was calm, we secured the boat
Next to a giant rock,
Then over the side we went, and swam
Toward that narrow gap,
Then dived below with the tidal flow
There was just the one mishap.

Jill caught her tank on the overhang
And it nicked her feeder hose,
She still had air, but I had to stare
As a stream of bubbles rose,
We swam right into the inner cave
Where the roof gave us more height,
So up we came to the air again
And I lit my small flashlight.

The walls reflected the sudden beam
In a thousand different ways,
There were reds and greens, and even cream
In a host of coloured sprays,
Then further on as we swam along
Was a ledge we clambered on,'
And there the bones of a longboat lay
From a time, both dead and gone.

And further in was a pile of bones
Of some poor, benighted soul,
Caught in hell in this prison cell
When the tide began to roll,
He must have come when the tide was low
And sailed in through the gap,
Then stayed too late, there was no escape
Once the tide had closed the trap.

And close by him lay an iron chest
With its bands all rusted through,
Full of coins, of gold Moidores
And Spanish Dollars too.
But Jill became so excited by
The glitter of the stuff,
That she'd forgotten the fractured hose,
Or to turn her Oxy off.

I played the light up above the bones
Where a script was scratched in the wall,
'God help me, I was cast in here
By the crew of the 'One for All,'
They told me to hide the treasure here
And would pick me up at eleven,
But then the entrance disappeared,'
It was '1797.'

Jill's tank was empty when we looked,
So I said I'd leave her there,
Go back and pick up another tank
But her face was filled with fear.
It's been a week since I left her there
For the sea's blown up, as well,
And the entrance to the cave has gone
Under a ten foot swell.

I'd give all the coin, and gold doubloons
Just to get my woman back,
But there's been a great white pointer there,
I'm afraid of a shark attack.
If she just can last till the sea goes down
I shall go to that awful cave,
But the thought I've fought since I left her there,
'It may be my woman's grave.'

The Eye of the Beast

I was strolling around the cemetery
On a Sunday afternoon,
When the crumbling earth had opened up
And I fell in a werewolf's tomb,
I wouldn't have thought it possible
Were it not for the werewolf's teeth,
That grazed my arm, and cut my hand,
It was way beyond belief.

But there it was with a canine head
And a slack and open jaw,
Just half a man and half a beast
With a mouth like the devil's maw,
Its teeth were sharp, serrated as
The blood ran down my arm,
Went mingling with the ancient fur
That had kept the creature warm.

I must have shrieked in the ancient grave
For they came to pull me out,
But once they noticed the wooden stake
Leapt back, with many a shout,
They all shrank back away from me
As if I was unclean,
And left me shivering by the grave
Like a leper in a dream.

And so I slunk back home again
Bent over in my shame,
I padded swiftly through the weeds
Like a dog that's going lame,

The blood had clotted along my arm
Had soaked right through my shirt,
So I thought that I'd better hide it then
By rolling in the dirt.

My spectacles were cracked by then
So I cast them off, aside,
I couldn't believe my vision, with
My eyes, so open wide,
I saw with pin-point clarity,
Not like I'd seen before,
When everything, both near and far
Was seen through a hazy blur.

My wife was sitting and waiting in
Her old and comfy chair,
And though she greeted me cheerily
I could only smell her hair,
But just one thing had startled me
And it's worthy now to note,
My eyes had sought out her jugular
Soft pulsing at her throat.

It didn't take me long to tell her
Why I felt unclean,
She bathed and smeared my hand and arm
With some white unguent cream,
Then in the kitchen, later on
Just as the Moon would rise,
She waved a jar of bright red blood
Right before my eyes.

'Now drink,' she said, 'drink every drop,
I know this ancient cure,
And I don't want to see you stop
Before I have you pure,'
And so I did, this cloying drink,
A foul and horrid taste,
And later on I found she'd made it
From tomato paste.

'There's lots of other condiments
I mixed into this crud,
I had to make you think that you
Were drinking human blood.'
'I'm cured of drinking blood for life
I said, 'how did you know?'
'My father was a werewolf too,
Some many years ago.'

Nowhere

How on earth did I arrive here
In this dark and dismal place,
When it all began with love, but
Of that love there's not a trace,
When you first began to spell me
I was helpless in your clutch,
Like an oak, you tried to fell me,
One who didn't matter much.

You would praise me up and raise me
When it suited you to play
With my juvenile emotions
You could have had me any day,

Though you never looked much further
Than the day that you would tire
Of your plaything, or the way things
Would consume me in your fire.

I was not more than a bangle or
A bracelet for your wrist,
You would get me so entangled that
I never could resist,
Then you tossed me in your tempests
Left me battling your storms,
Till you had me question love and
What it was, in all its forms.

Then you plunged me into darkness
Black as pitch, without a light,
And I wondered at this starkness
When you failed to say goodnight,
I have stumbled on your pathway
In my folly, now it seems,
But have missed the open gateway
In my search for love and dreams.

The Spectre

'It's coming in every night,' she said,
'And creeping across the floor,
It gives me an awful fright,' she said,
'Though I'm sure to lock the door.
I hear it shuffle, and then the creak
As it starts to climb the stair,
It stops outside on the landing then
And listens for me out there.'

'And I'm aware of my breathing then
As it's rattling in my throat,
I'm hiding under the covers when
I scream, in a long high note,
But still it's there and it tries the door
For the handle slowly turns,
Then I hear a 'pop' as my heart will stop,
As my face and my forehead burns.

'The door will creak on its hinges then
As it swings, and opens wide,
And I see a shadow dim and black
As it slowly comes inside,
I can't make out any features though
I think that it wears a cloak,
And a velvet mask of a black damask
As the scream dies in my throat.'

'It's like the Devil has come for me
Though it's way before my time,
I feel I'm starting to suffocate
In a coffin, filled with lime.
Oh why, Oh why don't you come for me
When I'm screaming in the gloom,
You're only just down the hallway
And asleep in another room.'

I sit by her and I pat her hand
And I make some soothing sounds,
I know why I'm never there for her
I'm coming in from the grounds,
I slide the key in the outer door
That she thinks I haven't got,
And creep on slowly up the stairs,
Whether she sleeps, or not.

I know that I'm mentioned in the will
That is under lock and key,
The house and all of its acres will
One day, devolve on me,
So I sit and soothe, and hold her hand
And I pat her on the back,
For one day soon, it won't be long
She'll die of a heart attack.

The Freak-Out Ghost

I've long been pondering suicide,
My life is such a mess,
I thought to try on the other side,
It couldn't be worse than this,
I'd always been such a coward though
My pain threshold is low,
I wondered how I could kill myself
With just one simple blow.

I didn't fancy to cut my throat
There's such a lot of blood,
And somebody has to clean it up
They'd curse me, as they should,
A gunshot straight to the head would put
My brains all over the wall,
And everything would be grey and red
With a blood-spray in the hall.

So I considered a poison pill
And a quart of Mister Beam,
That might just happen to fit the bill
For a death, both quick and clean,

But where would I get a poison pill
To accelerate my death?
I'd hate to die when I'm feeling ill,
Fighting for every breath.

I'd pondered on it so very long
That it quite obsessed my mind,
And I began to see shapes and figures
From some other time,
The ghosts of others who'd gone ahead
And done the evil deed,
Were poisoned, shot, or their throats were cut
When their own lives were in need.

They seemed to come when the clock struck twelve
Just on the midnight hour,
That's when the demons that rot in hell
Can demonstrate their power,
They kept on coming to egg me on
To get on that fatal bus,
'You need to do it, it isn't wrong,
You can join with all of us!'

They almost had me convinced that I
Could drown myself in the sea,
Or pick my favourite river then,
One that appealed to me,
They said to drown was a pleasant death
I'd drift away in a dream,
And none would know that I'd killed myself,
It's an 'accidental' theme.

The next night there came a stranger to
This ghostly neighbourhood,
Trailing festoons of river weed
And covered in clods of mud,
His face was twisted in anguish and
Such pain, that now I see,
Why I have suddenly changed my mind,
That freak-out ghost, was me!

The Muse

That wild energy that's the muse of the sea
When I loiter the beach in a storm,
Will always reflect all your features to me
As I dwell on the shape of your form.

I think of you striding knee deep in the swell
As the foam swirls and leaps at your thighs,
Above you the stars that will add to your spell
And reflect in the depth of your eyes.

For nature has laid some perfection on you
From the curl of your hair to your heels,
While I am caught up with an outsider's view
Of what nature's perfection reveals.

You're way beyond beauty, and way beyond touch
As your hair reflects acres of corn,
Your skin has a fragrance that's almost too much
From the moment perfection was born.

Your smile has a radiance hard to describe
As it peers down on me from above,
Its essence the finest of wines to imbibe
In its warmth, and the presence of love.

Beware of the man who has death in his soul
And the winter set deep in his eyes,
He'll court and he'll chaff you, until he can have you
Then tear you apart with his lies.

If I could but charm you, I'd never alarm you
But gaze on you rapt from afar,
Your love would be taken, but never forsaken
I'd worship you just as you are.

The Village of Crone

I went for a walk in a farmer's field
That once was a village street,
The cobbles were buried under the weeds
And scattering ears of wheat,
I wondered what had become of them,
Had they just faded away,
And left the buildings to tumble down
In disrepair and dismay?

Here the occasional chimney stood
Its flu still blackened with soot,
That once had shone with a rosy glow
Reflected by someone's foot.
And there the remains of a hearth still lay
Where mother had cooked the food,
And once there had been a child at play
Outside, where a swing had stood.

I found the remains of an old stone slab
Worn down by the passage of feet,
The entranceway to the Inn they had
In the days when life was sweet,
But something had come to sweep it away
To level it all to the ground,
And I was struck by the silence there,
Marked by the absence of sound.

I finally came to the cemetery
That sat alongside a wood,
A pitiful forest of standing stones
Each marked with a name, but crude,
And in the middle a pitch black stone
That sat at odds with the rest,
'Here lie the remains of the Witch of Crone,
May she burn in Hell, Bad Cess!'

It seemed then that the villagers had
Their taste of evil ways,
Before some force had hurried along
To see each building razed,
For then I stumbled across a stone
That lay, each shattered piece,
As if it was struck by lightning there
When he was just deceased.

I began to gather the pieces
Like a puzzle in that field,
And started to put it together,
See what secrets it would yield,
'Here lies the Village Witch Finder,' said
The sorry tale at last,
His name, 'Nathaniel Binder', carved
Before that final blast.

Then once that the tale was there to tell
I could hear a distant growl,
Deep in the wooded trees nearby
Like some grim and ancient howl,
And the black stone in that cemetery
Began to glow so bright,
As smoke poured off from its surface then,
Making me weak with fright.

I never went back to that farmer's field,
Or that vast, unholy ground,
But I passed just once the village pond,
A hole, and not to be found,
The earth had opened, swallowed it up
In a time of great despair,
And there by the edge of that ancient pond
The remains of the ducking chair.

The Dockyard Wife

He sat in the Bell & Lantern with
His pipe and with his beer,
The streets were wet on a misty night
With the pub, the only cheer,
He'd only married the month before
To a girl, not half his age,
And laid it out like a written law,
'You must make a living wage.'

He said that he'd been disabled by
A burst of cannon shot,
Unleashed by one of the Frenchmen
On his sloop, 'The Camelot'
He said that he'd done his duty by
His country and the King,
So she would have to support them both
By doing anything.

She wondered what he had meant at first
But soon was disabused,
When he ripped open her bodice, saying
'What you've got, you'll use.
There's sailors down at the docks each night
Who've been at sea too long,
They'll pay for a bit of comfort, girl,
I want you to be strong.'

He chose the most of her wardrobe and
He threw away her drawers,
He said, 'Whenever you greet one, you say,
'What is mine, is yours.'

He chose a long cotton dress, he said
Was much more like a shift,
'You have to be more than available,
It's easier to lift.'

He wouldn't be moved by the tears she shed,
How much she would implore,
His eyes were hard as her feelings bled,
His word would be the law,
He sent her out as the moon rose up
With its faint reflected light,
'Make sure you bring all the money back
When you're finished for the night.'

She wandered along dark alleyways
And she saw their shadow shapes,
Standing by darkened buildings, some
With caps and some with capes,
Their eyes would follow her down the lanes
Until just one would shout,
'Now there's the prettiest dolly bird,
What are you doing out?'

She'd soon get used to the smell of them,
Tobacco, gin and beer,
They'd come in close for a feel of her,
She'd try to hide her fear,
They'd ask how much for a little touch
She would say a shilling down,
If they were more of a gentleman
She would ask for half a crown.

Most of them took her standing up
With her dress up to her waist,
Or bent her over a barrel,
It depended all on taste,
She'd work right through to the midnight hour
It depended on the trade,
He'd ask in the Bell & Lantern just
How often she'd been laid.

A good night, often she'd bring a pound
That he'd put down on the bar,
And pay for a round of drinks for mates
And for her, a pot or jar,
She'd blush and sit in the corner while
They'd leer and peer and joke,
The bolder ones would approach him, ask
'How much for a friendly poke?'

He'd say, 'She's my little money box,
It will cost you half a quid,
But you must be nice, she's sugar and spice
And she'll tell me what you did.'
Then one might lay his money down, say
I'm feeling like a ride,
While he would laugh at his other half,
'You can take the girl outside.'

One night when out on the dockyard she
Looked bleakly up at the stars,
And saw the Moon through the mist and gloom
Sitting right next to Mars,
So back at the Bell & Lantern she
Picked up and shattered a glass,
Lunged up, and thrust it into his face,
With Mars in her eyes, at last.

The Village of Ghosts

I didn't have much to put down… He said,
'You wouldn't get much with that.'
I'd wanted to buy a cottage while
The housing market was flat.
With prices as low as they'd ever been
I thought I'd be in with a chance,
'Unless you go to that rustic show
The village of Experance.'

'The place has been empty for thirty years
With cottages up for a song,
There is no power, no place for a shower,'
But I thought I couldn't go wrong.
He drove me out to the village green,
Each garden was choked with weeds,
I'd buy most anything, sight unseen,``
As long as it suited my needs.

I picked one out with the roof intact
And the walls preserved with lime,
Some of the window panes were cracked,
I could fix them anytime.
The rooms were small, but overall
It would suit me down to a 'T',
I didn't have anyone in my life
I was single, young and free.

I brought what furniture I had left
And settled it down inside,
Then spent a week with a cleaning brush
It was just a question of pride.

I finally had my home sweet home
But lit with a paraffin lamp,
The water I drew from a well out back,
The walls were a trifle damp.

There wasn't another soul to be seen
They'd all moved away, or died,
I felt a little bit lonely there
But I walked the countryside.
I checked each cottage, the ancient hall
And the church, way down in the dell,
Someone had painted a cross on the door
And underlined it with 'Hell'.

One night I listened and heard a step
Out there on the path outside,
Got up and walked to the window, and
Out there was a beautiful bride.
She stood uncertain, unveiled her face
Her make-up was streaked with tears,
But when I opened the cottage door
The woman had disappeared.

I saw the groom on the following day
He stood by the next cottage down,
I waved, and thought he would look my way
But all that he did was frown.
He turned and entered the cottage door
But it didn't creak, or slam,
And when I looked, the weeds on the floor
Said empty, no sign of the man.

One night, I heard a sound in the hall
Like music and shuffling feet,
So wandered down, and stood by the wall
While lights shone out in the street,
But when I entered, the place was grim
And shrouded in silence and gloom,
I stood there shivering, on my own,
It felt like the depths of a tomb.

At night, I finally started to dream
And I saw the bride in her lace,
She came and tapped on my window pane
With tears streaming down her face,
'You have to come, a man with a gun,
Has shattered my wedding dream,'
I tossed and turned, until I awoke
Then pondered on what I'd seen.

One Sunday late, and fully awake
I wandered down to the church,
And by the time that I stood outside
I could hear the wedding march.
I pushed the door and it swung out wide
As I entered there in the gloom,
Then heard the sound of a pistol shot
That echoed across that room.

And just for a moment, they were there,
The spectres of what had been,
The wedding party standing in shock
As I looked at that terrible scene.
A shape ran past me, out at the door
As the bride let out a cry,
And there the groom, lay dead on the floor
With blood running out of his eye.

It faded then, and I was alone
In this dreadful church in the dell,
Where someone had painted a bright red cross
And underlined it with 'Hell'.
A curse must have come on the village that night
When the villagers all had cried,
For all that was left were the ghosts of death
From the night that the bridegroom died.

The Missing

What will I miss the most, I thought,
Now that she's not around,
I walked back slowly to the Port
With my face turned to the ground,
Would I miss the incessant chatter that
Would drive St. Peter mad?
Or sit with a sigh of pure relief
At the absence of it… Sad!

And what of the silly songs she sang
When I often used to curse,
Telling her that she'd got it wrong,
Forgotten the second verse,
For then she would just ignore me
And go out and feed the birds,
Singing the same old song again
But making up the words.

I'd ask her to wear the blue dress
So she'd go and wear the green,
The one that had such a diving top
That her cleavage was obscene,

She'd only do it to thwart we when
We'd visit with my kin,
Annoying my strait-laced mother,
'How on earth do you keep them in?'

She was just the size of a hobbit, or
A tiny little sprite,
Would lie with her back towards me
When we cuddled up at night,
Those were the things that I would miss
I thought, with just a tear,
Why did she have to leave me at
The turning of the year?

Christmas never would be the same,
She'd decorate the tree,
Getting the lights a-blinking which
Was more than they did for me,
I entered the door at home, and listened,
Nary a single sound,
And never would be again, now she
Was planted in the ground.

A Question of Fate

You only can die but once, they say,
There isn't a second time,
We carry fears all along the years
When we think, which day is mine?
We envisage that marble headstone
That's indicative of our fate,
Standing erect in some unknown field,
And wonder about the date.

How often we hear that someone said
While trying to be more than brave,
But shuddering at the thought of the dead,
'Someone just walked on my grave.'
It creeps on up, the length of your spine
The shiver that never ends,
Bringing a list of your sins to mind
With no time to make amends.

You think of that open casket,
And lying there sightlessly,
So all can stare, and look at you there,
'I'm glad that it isn't me.'
We wonder if we will hear them sigh
About all the good we did,
Or even know, if terror will grow
The moment they close the lid.

I think about Averill Crombie
Who said that she knew the date,
And suddenly died as she sat wide-eyed
Poking the fire in the grate.
We all went along to the service,
To say our goodbyes, as we should,
But then our hair, stood up in the air,
On hearing three taps on the wood.

We scrambled to open the coffin,
To find her still breathing in there,
And then she began to start coughing,
Sucking in lungfuls of air.

She tried to climb out of the casket
With many a cuss and a curse,
But then must have blown a gasket,
So we carried her into the hearse.

You only can die but once, they say,
There isn't a second time,
She knew the date, it was simply fate
But the first time blew her mind.
I still see them lower her into the ground
When she'd died, just twice, perhaps,
But I couldn't swear, when leaving her there
That there weren't three ghostly taps.

The Black Freighter

The Cormorant was the darkest ship,
As dark as a ship could be,
Not only the paint was pitted black
From the funnels to the sea,
But deep inside in its rusted gloom
In the echoes from its shell,
It was like a monster roamed abroad
Released from the depths of hell.

It roared and echoed by day and night
As the boilers turned the screw,
Lurching across every wave that might
Try to break its hull in two,

It was laden down with a thousand tons
Of a cargo that made it groan,
While breakers slapped its quivering sides
As it made its way back home.

The Captain stood on the shuddering bridge,
A man with a heart of steel,
He tried to control this raging beast
As he lashed himself to the wheel,
He gave no quarter to any man
Who would shirk, avoid his task,
But called the crew to witness his due
As the man was soundly lashed.

Down in the depths of the engine room
The firemen shovelled coal,
Each shovel sprayed like a black dismay
In the light of that glowing hole,
And steam built up on the pressure gauge
Of each boiler, one and two,
As men would fret, while running in sweat,
To do what they had to do.

The seas built up and the rain came down
As the Cormorant rolled and swayed,
Then lightning flashed and it ran to ground
Like an imp in a masquerade,
It left three dead on the afterdeck,
They hurried to help them there,
But the captain roared, 'Throw them overboard,
We've more than enough to spare.'

A mutter grew up among the crew
As dark as the bosun's hat,
I never knew what the crew would do
So I wasn't in on that.
But the Captain disappeared from the bridge
And the wheel was swinging free,
With the Cormorant broadside to the waves
At mercy of wind and sea.

They said it must be a miracle
When we finally entered port,
The bilge half full of water, they said,
And the Captain fell overboard.
But the ship was done, had made its last run
As the fires went out in the hull,
Then raking through the mountain of ash
I found the late Captain's skull.

Go Out and Anchor the Boat

The cumulus clouds built overhead
But were dark, and filled with rain,
They brought to the sky a sense of dread
Of the storm to come, and pain,
The wind picked up in the barley fields
And the sea beat in to the shore,
'If you don't go out and anchor the boat
It will land on the rocks, for sure.'

I didn't want to go out that day
But my father said I must,
All that my brother did was play
So I thought it so unjust.
'Why is it always me,' I said,
'When Fred's as handy as I,
He only goes when the weather's calm
With not a cloud in the sky.'

It made no odds so I had to go,
They didn't give me a choice,
I was the child of the family,
The one with the weakest voice.
I took the skip and I rowed on out
Where the Huntsman strained its chain,
With the breakers crashing across the prow
On top of the driving rain.

I seized the rope and clambered aboard
Then tied the skip to a post,
It was only held by a slender cord
To the Huntsman, as its host.
I went for the starboard anchor then
And slipped it into the sea,
That would give it a second hold, I thought,
But in truth, there should be three.

The waves were crashing across the deck
And the Huntsman wheeled around,
Now side-on to the waves it heeled
With a rasping, creaking sound,
If only Fred hadn't lost the anchor
Chained up close to the bow,
I would be able to hold the swing
But it wasn't likely now.

The swell was something tremendous and
The rain came down like sleet,
What with the sway and the decks awash
It was hard to keep my feet.
Slowly the boat had begun to drift and
Drag its chains to the shore,
Down in a trough, and then the lift
As the swell built up once more.

Making my way to the cabin door
I locked myself inside,
Then started the Perkins diesel and
Prepared to go for a ride,
I thought that if I could turn the bow
And point it out to sea,
We might be able to ride it out
The boat, brute force, and me.

I didn't know that my brother Fred
Had borrowed somebody's skiff,
And now was heading on out to help,
My father had said ,'What if?'
The diesel roared into life and tugged
The anchors in its wake,
But wouldn't respond to the rudder
I had made my first mistake.

Borne on the swell, the Huntsman roared
And headed in to land,
Nothing I did would turn the bow
Though I had the wheel in hand,
I'll never live down the Huntsman's loss
Or forget that awful sound,
That terrible scream like a nightmare dream
As I ran my brother down.

The Sacrifice

They took her up to the mountain top
With the altar set in place,
I screamed and shouted for them to stop,
But they laughed, spat in my face.
They threatened me as they laid her down
On that cold grey marble slab,
Then stripped the clothes from her shivering form
As I told them they were mad.

She lay exposed for the world to see
As they formed a line around,
So grim they looked in their livery
In their hoods, and long black gowns,
I wasn't part of their magic cell
And they said I'd have to leave,
Before enacting their secret spell
That would leave me then to grieve.

'You're just a pack of barbarians,'
I shrieked, but the mood was tense,
'Go play with your Rastafarians,'
They laughed, but it made no sense,
Why would they murder an innocent girl
In the third phase of the moon,
Just to appease some devilish god
On the first Sunday in June.

Two hulking brutes took a-hold of me
And they dragged me down the hill,
I said, 'you're all going to pay for this,
You're denying my free will.'

They left me there and they climbed back up
But they'd said, 'You'd best beware,
You might be a second sacrifice
Should you try to come back there.'

I heard their horrible mumble as
The group began to chant,
It came in waves from the hilltop graves
Like some evil covenant,
But then the scream of a four wheel drive
Came roaring up the hill,
Filled with the men in uniform
I can see the vision still.

Three shots rang out, there was quite a rout
As the hoods had turned to flee,
Stumbling down the mountainside
And a few had passed by me,
I wondered then who had brought them there
To defeat this evil scheme,
It's beyond belief, but I felt relief
When the girl began to scream.

A year has flown, but I'm not alone
Since they saved that sacrifice,
She's home and free, and she married me,
And I must admit, it's nice.
I've often said, 'What was in your head,
When you turned to me,' and stuff,
'I thought I might as well marry you
Since you saw me in the buff.'

The Little Toy Shop

The little Toy Shop in the High Street,
With its pebble glass windows and doors,
Was a magical place, with its curtains of lace
And delight on its shelves and its floors.
It had always enticed and enthralled me,
With its skaters that whirled on a rink,
With tops that would hum, and soldiers with drum,
And dolls with bright eyes that would blink.

It had stood near the kerb in the High Street
In a small seaside village in Wales,
And we would go there for a part of the year
Near the Inn that was selling Welsh ales.
And I would stare in through the window
Though the glass would distort what I'd see,
When the women would pass, all the chattering class
I would think they were talking to me.

It would sound like they sang to each other,
Not a word in my English was said,
And their voices would meld with that Toy Shop,
Till I thought, 'What goes on in their head?'
But I left that Welsh village behind me
As I grew, with much laughter and tears,
It was later, a trip would remind me,
What I'd left in the past, all those years.

Then I found myself standing outside it,
That little Toy Shop from the past,
Where nothing had changed, just the stock rearranged
When I stared through that window at last.

I opened the door with the pebble glass
And I made my way slowly within,
And there stood a girl in a bonnet and blouse
And a pinny tucked all the way in.

Her hair was the colour of seaside sand
And her eyes were the blue of the sea,
I noticed that there was no ring on her hand
And that she stared intently at me.
I think we both knew in an instant then
That within a short year we'd be wed,
But though she still sings in her Welsh with a friend
I don't know what goes on in her head.

Home to Roost

The mornings were cold and dreary when
We used to meet at the Kirk,
And you would be sad and teary on
The blustery days to work,
I'd ask you why you were sad and drawn
But you usually pulled a face,
And knowing you, it was him again,
Your husband, what a disgrace!

I never could understand how you
Had chosen him over me,
He wouldn't work in an iron lung
But had a 'need to be free.'
I knew he wouldn't look after you
But you were blind as a bat,
You didn't even react when you
Had caught him, kicking your cat.

I knew that he had a violent side,
You said that it wasn't true,
'He's always so warm and loving.'
'Yes,' I said, 'till he turns on you.'
But nevertheless you married him
And it's been now almost a year,
Whenever we make our way to work
You're never without a tear.

I cornered him in a midnight bar
He was more than a little drunk,
I said that he'd better treat you fair
And called him a low-life skunk,
He took a swing and I laid him out
Now you're never to talk to me,
I see you now and you look away
So our friendship's not to be.

On Monday, you had a broken cheek
And wore make-up on that eye,
I took you down to the hospital
And I watched you sit and cry,
I swore by God I would get revenge
While he drank at the local bar,
I took some snips and a couple of nips
As I doctored up his car.

Now God in heaven forgive me
Though I did what I had to do,
I need you so to believe me for
I'd not meant to injure you,
You met him there at the bar that night
As my heart was in my mouth,
And climbed aboard, and you hit the road
On the highway, headed south.

I followed some way behind you, and
I really had the shakes,
The oncoming lights would blind you
Then I saw him hit the brakes,
He ran off the road and hit the tree
And you both went through the screen,
I've never seen so much blood before
And I knew I'd lost my dream.

I'm standing beside your coffin in
That tiny little Kirk,
The one where we met on Sundays, and
Before we went to work,
No matter how violent he had been
I'd played too fast and loose,
And though he was dead, I knew in my head,
Our sins had come home to roost.

Twilight

I look for you in the twilight glow
When the sun dips over the rim,
When it's night time here and it's daytime there
And I think of you there with him.
Though you said, 'It's just for a holiday,
And I promise that I'll be good,'
Well I'm sure you were, as he stroked your hair
In the shade of the underwood.

Whenever the twilight's coming on
And the Moon moves up in the sky,
I sit and dream in a cold moonbeam
And mull over the question, 'Why?'

You said that you had two itchy feet
In a sense, they wanted to roam,
And though you were trying to be discreet
I knew you were leaving home.

So now I sit, and cry in the dark
Of the twilight's utter gloom,
And think of you in a pleasure park
Where you flew on your witches broom.
I know you couldn't be on your own
I can see the dark shape of him,
He's there when you ought to be alone
As you taste of the fruits of sin.

The sun peers over the morning rim
As I bid goodbye to the night,
And see where I shattered the mirror in
That I look like a sleepless fright.
The silence shrieks with a telephone ring,
As I answer it, you say:
'I'm looking forward to coming home,'
And, 'Thanks for the holiday!'

Flight of the Crows

We were out on a training mission
Up in a Neptune, hunting a sub,
The pilot was Captain Grissom
Taking a nap, aye, that was the rub,
The plane was on auto-pilot
Left in the hands of Lieutenant Free,
While I was down in the nose cone
Keeping a watch, beneath us the sea.

The skies were a starlit wonder
Never a cloud to temper the view,
The Moon, it had barely risen
Casting its light with a purple hue,
We'd dropped right down to a thousand feet
As the sonar checked the bay,
Then Free had said, 'There's a flock of birds,
Just a couple of miles away.'

The plotters gave out a chatter
Picking the signals up from the buoys,
The Snifter, it didn't matter
It was detecting diesel oils,
But up on the pilot's radar screen
Was a mass of darkened rows,
I heard Free say on the intercom:
'It's a swarm of migrant crows.'

We knew we'd better not hit them
They could be sucked into the pods,
And then if they clogged the jets our fate
Would be in the hands of gods,

I peered on out through the perspex cone
It was much too dark to see
A couple of thousand crows out there
With feathers as black as could be.

Free said we should duck beneath them
So he took us down real low,
The shapes had massed on the radar screen
There couldn't be far to go,
And then I had caught a sight of them
The first of these flying things,
My voice croaked into the intercom,
'None of these crows have wings.'

They flew on the straight and level
Bunched in groups of two or three,
I knew they were something nasty,
Then I heard Lieutenant Free,
He seemed to choke, he's a rational bloke
And couldn't believe his eyes,
'If you can see what they are, tell me,
Don't give me a bunch of lies.'

But who'd be the first to say it,
I was pensive, down in the cone,
Nothing I'd say would mend it
If I was first to say on my own,
'It looks like a flight of witches
All in black, and each on a broom,'
The crew back there were in stitches
Thinking that I was a Looney Toon.

The coven dived on an island
Covered in trees, and out in the bay,

I thought that we might collect one
But we gave them the right of way,
'We'll tell them, when we get back,' said Free,
That it was a flight of crows,
Don't anyone talk about witches, for
It's best if nobody knows.'

The Smuggler

We went to live in Smuggler's Cove
Near a cave, right on the beach,
Where once they'd hidden ill-gotten gains
In the cave, and out of reach.
The locals said two hundred years
Since the smugglers came ashore,
Carrying casks of Spanish wine
And a chest of gold moidores.

Led by a man called One-Eye Red
For the only one he'd got,
He'd lost the other, the locals said,
To a random pistol shot,
He wore a patch on the missing eye
For the wind blew in at the hole,
And froze his brain till he went insane
When the winter winds were cold.

He hung with Sally, a thatcher's wife
Who would meet him in the cove,
And he would sample her plain delights
Till the time came round to rove.

She kept lookout on the cliff top there
For a glimpse of Revenue Men,
And would fire her flintlock pistol where
She had thought she'd sighted them.

My wife, her name was Sally too
And I'd rib her there in jest,
'You'd better not hug a smuggler, Sally,
Dressed only in your vest.'
We'd laugh back then in those early days
As we worked to settle in,
But sensed some dread foreboding there,
In the air from old past sin.

It came on strong in the winter time
When the cove was filled with mist,
The mouth of the cave was grim and dark
It would almost seem possessed,
Then Sally started to walk at night
As the waves crashed into the shore,
She said she needed to beat the fright
That she'd suffered from times before.

I'd watch her walk to the darkened cave
Then halt to stare in the mouth,
It opened onto the northern shore
Then she'd turn, and wander south,
She'd come back shivering, pale and wan
And would warm up by the fire,
Then come out with the strangest thing
That it filled her with desire.

She'd strip right off by the glowing hearth
And I'm not one to complain,
She'd not been so very down to earth
Since the Lord invented rain,
Then one night when the mist was thick
I could barely see the cave,
When a ghostly figure stepped from the sea
And walked all over my grave.

Then Sally turned and she spoke to him
As my stomach churned inside,
They walked together into the cave
Like a bridegroom and a bride,
I left the cottage, the door ajar
And I ran down to the beach,
But when I got to the mouth of the cave,
Sally was out of reach.

Sally was out of reach that day
And has been each day since,
The phantom that walked her into the cave
Was One-Eye Red at a pinch.
I called and called for her to come back,
I even tried to insist,
But all that I've seen on a winter's night
Are their shadows, abroad in the mist.

The Waif

She was walking the damp and cobbled streets
Like one with nowhere to go,
I saw her quivering, cold and shivering
Deep in a fall of snow,
I rarely talk to a stranger, but
She looked me straight in the eye,
And said, 'Dear sir, could you help a girl,
I noticed you passing by.'

She took me out of my comfort zone,
She quite appealed to the eye,
I mumbled in an embarrassed tone,
I have been known to be shy.
'I've not been warm for a week,' she said,
'And haven't slept, and I'm tired,
I wonder if you could take me home
And let me sit by your fire?'

I didn't want to be compromised,
I had a girl of my own,
But barely thinking, I said all right
And so she followed me home.
I built the fire with a log or two
Then she sat down by the grate,
And held her hands to the warming flames,
But the hour was getting late.

I wondered where she would sleep that night
With nowhere to go, she said,
Then like a fool, broke the golden rule
Said she could sleep in my bed.

'I'll stay out here on the couch, so you
Can catch right up on your sleep,'
If only I'd had a crystal ball
The future would make me weep.

She said that her name was Elspeth Jane,
Had run away from her home,
So stayed wherever there was no pain
From brutes, just bad to the bone.
She said she could tell a gentleman
And smiled, when looking at me,
I felt quite flattered, I must confess,
Not knowing what was to be.

I had a girl, and her name was Kate,
She'd be around in the morning,
I thought that the waif would be gone by then
But Kate showed as it was dawning.
'Who is the girl, there in your bed?'
As Elspeth lay a-bed, stretching,
'I thought I could trust you, now you're dead,'
Then Elspeth said I was letching.

'He picked me up for a bit of fun,
He didn't mention a girlfriend,
He's quite a lover, son of a gun,
You should hang on to your boyfriend.'
'Why would you lie, you slept alone,'
I looked in horror at Elspeth,
The door then slammed, and Kate had flown,
While Elspeth asked about breakfast.

I should have kicked her out in the street,
I should have barred her forever,
But first I offered her toast to eat,
Then thought it was now or never.
She walked back in through the bedroom door
Her gown slipped down off her shoulder,
I knew that a starving man must eat,
And now, I'm wiser and bolder.

The Seduction

She raked through the hearth fire ashes,
And scattered the chicken bones,
Then turned a page in a silent rage
And added some pebble stones.
She searched for a spell to end in hell
For the man who had told her 'No,'
A spell of hate from her hearth fire grate
To follow wherever he'd go.

While he stood out on the roadway
Considering where he'd been,
He'd fled out there from the witches lair
Where she'd lured him, sight unseen.
At first she seemed to be beautiful
When first he entered her lair,
But then his eyes grew wide in surprise,
Got used to the dark in there.

She'd sat on a velvet cushion
And raised her skirt to the knee,
He thought he saw what she wanted him for
As she smiled unpleasantly,

He turned in a mild confusion,
His women were never so bold,
He sat and stared, got out of his chair,
Said 'Sorry, you're just too old.'

He looked at the streets about him,
And noticed the cobblestones,
They crissed and crossed, he was more than lost
In a muddle of chicken bones.
He couldn't figure which way to go,
As they'd twist and turn out there,
And every time he would cross the road
He'd end back at the witches lair.

His mouth was a pile of ashes,
His mind full of pebble stones,
He found himself at the same front door
Spitting out chicken bones.
He burst back into the witches lair
And he saw her crouched by the hearth,
She stared at him with an awful grin,
Let out a terrible laugh.

'Have you come again to reject me,
To tell me I'm just too old?
You'll never recover your other lover,'
She said, and his heart turned cold.
He snatched at her faded Grimoire,
And turned to another page,
Then read a spell from a demon of hell
That was said, would make her age.

He muttered the words of the ritual
And her face grew taut with fear,
Her hair turned grey at the words he'd say
At the spell she'd not want to hear.
Her skin grew slack, and fell from her bones
As it said in that ancient tome,
Then his head had cleared as she disappeared,
And he went wandering home.

The Grange

They said that The Grange was a haunted house,
I said, 'you're having me on!'
But no, they said, 'he's back from the dead,'
I thought it a giant con.
'Just spend one night in that house alone
With the power cut off, you'll see,'
I said, 'I'll go, if Carolyn goes,
If Carolyn stays with me.'

Now she was more of a nervous type
But she said, 'I'll go with you,
Just promise you won't make whooshing sounds,
There's nothing a ghost can do.'
'There isn't a ghost,' I told her then,
They're all just having us on,
We'll spend the night, if you feel uptight
I'll prove that it's just a con.'

We ventured in through the cobwebbed porch
As the hour was getting late,
The only light we had was a torch
And the fire we lit in the grate,

The Moon came presently shining in
Its ghostly beam through the gloom,
And Carolyn came and cuddled up
As we sat on the floor of the room.

'Where did they say the ghost would be,'
She asked, as I patted her hair,
I couldn't say, I was miles away,
Then we heard a creak on the stair.
I thought, 'Oh no, it will spoil the show,'
I was hoping for just one kiss,
For this was the first time, she and I
Had ever been close, like this.

Then from above there were creaks and groans,
It came stumbling down the stair,
It looked like a bundle of rags and moans
And a skull, with eyes that glare,
Carolyn screamed as it reached for her
This thing from another world,
It bubbled and rasped in its throat, and said
One word that I think was 'Girl'.

It must have remembered from days before
It had held a girl like this,
Death had never erased the thought,
Or the feeling that was bliss,
But now, the rags of the grave were foul
It gave off a graveyard stench,
And Carolyn, all she could do was howl,
This alive and lovely wench.

What seemed to me an apparition
A ghost in empty air,
Was rotting flesh and bones to Carolyn
Tangled in her hair,
It held her in a grip of steel
As it probed beneath her dress,
I couldn't even fight it off
For to me, it was stagnant breath.

They came to us in the dawning light
With a key to let us out,
I lay as in a palsied dream
But I heard them scream and shout,
'What have you done to Carolyn,'
But they were to late to save,
For she had gone where the ghost had gone,
To join him in the grave.

The Final Party

He'd lain in the septic, hospital bed,
Was terminal, slipping away,
'He won't last forever,' the nurses said,
'Will probably go today.'
So they put him on a morphine drip
To ease the man of his plight,
'He looks so grey, and is on his way,
I think he'll be dead tonight.'

But deep in the slumbering fellow's head
There wasn't a shred of gloom,
A party was raging within his bed,
And filling that hospital room,

There were friends and folk he'd always known,
A neighbour he knew as Jim,
And there in a party dress, on her own,
That wonderful girl called Kim.

Would she even give him a second glance
He'd thought, in a sort of dread,
He'd seen her first at the village dance,
And now she was deep in his head.
Her lips were full and her eyes were brown
And her teeth were even and white,
He thought that his courage might let him down
Then swore, 'she'll be mine tonight.'

He nodded his head to a favourite tune
As tremors invaded his pillow,
Balloons were popping all through the room,
He stood by a favourite willow,
And Kim was paddling in the brook
That bubbled and babbled, madly,
He took a breath and a long last look,
He knew that he wanted her badly.

She turned and smiled, and walked to his bed,
And gave her lips to be kissed there,
She shimmered and swayed as his vision fled
And he stood alone by her grave there,
His smile was soft as the lights went out
And a nurse looked over him gravely,
'At last he's gone, I knew him as John,
He went to the other side bravely.'

They stripped his bed and they laid him out,
'I remember his wife,' one sighed,
'Her name was Kim, and she doted on him,
It must be a year since she died.'
'Who knows what happens to those who pass,'
A nurse said, folding the sheeting,
'I'd like to think they're together at last,
If just for a moment, fleeting…'

The Train with a Tender Heart

The train chugged on in the darkness
Past meadows and cattle asleep,
And the night revealed its starkness
Puffing smoke on the backs of sheep,
Its livery was as black as the soot
That covered its ageing paint,
It couldn't be classed as beautiful,
Though it might have been thought as quaint.

The night was such an inky black
As a cloud obscured the stars,
The train was sensing a nothingness
In the vast expanse to Mars,
The fireman sprayed its feed of coal
As the boiler felt the strain,
As tired pistons and tired wheels
Drove on the exhausted train.

A thought came out of the empty sky
And mixed with the sulphur stream,
'Why can't I be like the other trains
That little boys love, and dream,

Instead, I've spent my whole life long
Tied to an endless rail,
I've done all the driver wanted to
But I may as well be in jail.'

There was only an empty signal box
Unmanned at that time of night,
And miles and miles of dark ahead
With never a single light,
So an angry feeling was building up
At that Great Train in the sky,
That only commanded, 'what thou shalt,'
But never explained, 'but why?'

So into the dark it chugged along
With carriages in its wake,
While deep inside, the fireman asked
'Did anyone fix the brake?
The driver shook his gnarled old head
As if in a quick reply,
'There hasn't been time for the loco shed,
But they'll fix it, by and by.'

The boiler started to grumble so
They stopped at a water trough,
The fireman pulled the spout across
And turned it on, then off,
They pulled away with the tender full
Though the train was feeling pain,
'I'm always doing the same old thing,
I'm not going to stop again.'

So on they steamed to Hunterdown
Where at last the brakes had failed,
All they got was a steady scream
As the wheels spun on the rails,
And though the driver cut the steam
Still along the track it sped,
While the driver and the fireman
On the footplate, stood in dread.

'The rail runs out at Dead Man's Eye
Said the driver to his mate,
If we can't slow down this blessed thing,
I'm afraid, it's much too late.'
They chose to jump as the rail ran out
But the train still plunged ahead,
Over the untamed landscape
Riding on meadow grass instead.

The carriages piled behind it
Were detached in an awful wreck,
But still the locomotive drove
On a joyous final trek,
It rambled over a grassy ridge
And fell over a pleasant hill,
Next to a colourful flower bed,
And today, it lies there still.

Now children gather to play on it
This pile of rusted steel,
A train that had a tender heart
And for once could see and feel,
If all of its life were memories
Then the one it's surely got,
Is riding unfettered across the green
To a bed of forget-me-nots.

Storm Island

We ran aground on an island,
In the eye of a hurricane,
The wind was swirling around us,
As loud as a runaway train,
A dozen people had floated up
Sucked off the deck of the ship,
Lost forever in giant seas
At the height of our pleasure trip.

The ship was battered and spun around
Like a toy in the hands of a boy,
This giant behemoth of the seas
Tossed round like a tinker toy.
We heard it grind on the outer reef
Then be driven right up to the beach,
It slowly toppled, onto its side
With the lifeboats out of reach.

We hid inside till the storm was spent
Then cautiously went ashore,
There must have been a hundred of us,
But there had been hundreds more,
Some drowned in the lower cabins
When the sides of the ship were breached,
And others died, fell over the side
As the priest of the ship had preached.

But there was no god in the heavens,
Just the mighty god of the storm,
We were soaked, and so dishevelled,
Just trying to keep us warm,

So we sheltered in a grove of trees
That had swayed, but still they stood,
While the men went through the fallen trees
Gathering firewood.

It was night before we knew it,
There had been torrential rain,
The many fires that we had lit
Were lit, and lit again,
We managed a palm frond shelter
To protect us from the breeze,
But people were dying, by the score
With old men on their knees.

If only the ship had stayed upright
We could treat it like a shack,
But once we found we were on the ground
There was no way to climb back,
And then at night we were all in fright
When we heard a roar, so bold,
Like a raging beast in the further trees
That it made our blood run cold.

People were screaming in the dark
On the outskirts of the crowd,
And sounds of ripping, and gnashing teeth
In the darkness were so loud,
The morning showed us the grisly truth
There were pieces everywhere,
Whatever it was, and to our cost
They'd been sounds of rip and tear.

That only leaves a dozen of us
So I cast this into the sea,
A scrawl in a tiny bottle in
The hopes that you'll set us free.
We take it in turns to keep a watch
For the monster of this shore,
On this tiny little island that
Has never been mapped before.

Sally Ann

'Where are you going, Sally Ann
Now the nights have become so dark,
Why do you get so restless, say
You want to walk in the park?'
I thought to sit by the fireside
Each time that she ventured out,
It's cold and damp by the streetlight lamp,
So what was it all about?

'I need to go where the wind will blow,
Feel the damp caressing my cheek,
The bracing air is a tonic there,
While you sit, and you never speak.
It gets so terribly warm in here,
I feel I can barely breathe,
You sit and enjoy your fireside chair
But me, I just have to leave.'

So I'd go and stare out the window
Just as she left, my Sally Ann,
The thought was crossing my mind just then
Was she meeting some other man?
The question sat on my lips at times
But I thought I'd better not say,
If once I questioned my Sally Ann
It might just drive her away.

I'd watch her stand at the kerbside edge
And ponder which way to go,
She'd walk by the village of Kirby Ledge
Or left, round the bungalow,
It happened often she'd cross the road
And wander off to the mill,
I knew she'd get to the park that way
The other side of the hill.

One night, the rain it came pelting down
I knew she'd be good and wet,
I went to the old umbrella stand
And thought I could catch her yet,
The wind was gusting, the rain blew in,
In flurries under my hood,
I barely could see the way she'd been,
In passing by Farley Wood.

I saw the light of a dim-lit torch
Flashing under the trees,
And wandered over to take a look
Though feeling weak in the knees,
A woman lay on a groundsheet there
Though he had covered her face,
I still could see that her limbs were bare
And thrashing all over the place.

147

'Oh Sally Ann,' I had sobbed, and ran,
While making my way back home,
I cursed the folly of coming out,
It was better I hadn't known.
Then Sally Ann had opened the door
Said 'Come in out of the rain.
I went to walk but I cut it short.'
I flew to her arms again.

Gone Shopping

I'm sitting here in the morning glow
Of the early winter sun,
Staring at the picture of you
And wondering what I've done,
You left to go on a shopping trip
In the middle of the week,
You said that you'd be an hour away
Was the last I heard you speak.

I'm used to you never turning up
So I knew I'd have to wait,
I've often taken a chair out there
To sit by the garden gate,
The sun went down and the Moon came up
There was still no sign of you,
And when I crawled upstairs I saw
That the bed was empty too.

I wondered what you were shopping for
As it's true, you never tell,
You might be looking for pitchforks from
The seventh circle of hell,
You come back home with the strangest things
Like a bag of knitted straw,
And once with a dozen rubber rings
What did you want them for?

A day went by and I rang around,
Caught up with your friend Denise,
Checked with the local hospital,
With the Firemen and the Police,
But nobody knew just where you were
Or at least, they wouldn't say,
Constable Gurk suppressed a smirk
Said you might have run away.

Somebody said that you'd passed them by
In a number fourteen bus,
Another one said, they don't know why,
You were seen with Uncle Gus.
I knew all along that must be wrong
Though I don't know why they lied,
They must have been seeing things, it's been
A year since my Uncle died.

So now I'm left with a mystery
It's already been a week,
I've been so alone, all on my own
I'm forgetting how to speak.
I'd never have thought you'd want to leave
I thought that our love was true,
I've just had a call, you'd not believe,
They found you, locked in the Zoo.

150

www.ingramcontent.com/pod-product-compliance
Lightning Source LLC
LaVergne TN
LVHW051640080426
835511LV00016B/2417